AMERICAN IRIDESCENT
Stretch Glass

IDENTIFICATION & VALUE GUIDE

FENTON • NORTHWOOD •U.S. GLASS
IMPERIAL • DIAMOND • VINELAND
LANCASTER • CENTRAL • JEANNETTE

John Madeley & Dave Shetlar

COLLECTOR BOOKS
A Division of Schroeder Publishing Co., Inc.

MW01079123

The current values in this book should be used only as a guide. They are not intended to set prices, which vary from one section of the country to another. Auction prices as well as dealer prices vary greatly and are affected by condition as well as demand. Neither the Authors nor the Publisher assumes responsibility for any losses that might be incurred as a result of consulting this guide.

Searching for a Publisher?

We are always looking for knowledgeable people considered to be experts within their fields. If you feel that there is a real need for a book on your collectible subject and have a large comprehensive collection, contact Collector Books.

On the front cover:
Top right: Bowl, #603, three-footed, crimped, Celeste Blue, 10⅜"w, 5¼"h, 2⅞"b, $275.00. Fenton Art Glass Company. (See other color, Plate 135.)
Middle left: Candy Jar, #835, ½-lb, Tangerine, 4¼"w, 9½"h, 3"b, $80.00. Fenton Art Glass Company.
Middle right: Bowl, #8076, Open Work, flared, flat rim, Pearl Blue (opaque blue slag), 11⅛"w, 2¼"h, 3¾"b, rare color, $300.00. United States Glass Company.
Bottom left: Console Set, Green with "glue chip" etching and gold decoration, rare decoration; Bowl, rolled rim, 9"w, 3½"h, 3½"b; Candlesticks, 7¼"h, 4"b, $150.00 set. Central Glass Works.
Bottom right: Vase, #693, Amethyst Ice (purple), 5¼"w, 10¾"h, 3½"b, $100.00. Imperial Glass Company.

On the back cover:
Top: Vanity Set, #54, Persian Pearl (crystal) with decoration, rare shape, $460.00 set; Cologne, 1½"w, 5"h, 1¾"b, $130.00; Puff Box, 4¼"w, 3¾"h, 2½"b, $80.00; Tray, 5⅞" x 8½"w, ⅝"h, $120.00. Fenton Art Glass Company.
Middle: Bowl, cupped, red, 8"w, 3¾"h, 4"b, $150.00. Diamond Glass-Ware Company.
Bottom: Pitcher and Tumbler Set, 10 pieces with coasters, Blue $430.00 set; Pitcher, covered, diamond optic, 4"w, 11¾"h, 4⅝"b, $250.00; Tumblers, diamond pattern, 3¼"w, 4⅝"h, 2⅜"b, $30.00 each; Coasters, #5, cobalt not iridized, 3¼"w, ⅜"h, $15.00 each. H. Northwood and Company.

Cover design: Beth Summers
Book design: Sherry Kraus

COLLECTOR BOOKS
P.O. Box 3009
Paducah, Kentucky 42002–3009

Copyright © 1998 by John Madeley & Dave Shetlar

All rights reserved. No part of this book may be reproduced, stored in any retrieval system, or transmitted in any form, or by any means including but not limited to electronic, mechanical, photocopy, recording, or otherwise, without the written consent of the authors and publisher.

Contents

Acknowledgments

This book represents our efforts to compile a concise and complete listing of American stretch glass currently known to us. We could not have completed this work without the assistance and support of numerous fellow stretch glass collectors.

Our guiding goal has been to provide fellow stretch glass collectors and collectors of similar glassware made by the stretch glass manufacturers a means of identifying much of the common "tableware" made from 1916 to the early 1930s. Stretch glass is still being made today, mainly by the Fenton Art Glass Company. Though we have included a few pieces of these modern productions, this book is primarily intended to help identify the old pieces.

Most of our knowledge of stretch glass lines, colors, and manufacturers has been learned through the kind and patient teachings of expert glass historians and researchers. At the top of our list is Berry Wiggins, co-author of numerous glass books and tireless researcher. Frank M. Fenton has also been generous to share his knowledge of glass making and manufacturers. Bill Crowl also gets a special thanks since his travels across the United States to gather glassware have brought to light many pieces of stretch glass which he has shared with the authors.

Since our patience is too short to camp out in the Library of Congress, the Corning Museum of Glass, and other repositories of glass information, most of the short accounts of the various companies that made stretch glass come from the numerous books on these specific glass companies. We certainly encourage readers who quest for historical information on these companies to invest in these books. We rest most of our compiled knowledge on the works of William Heacock, James Measell, Berry Wiggins, Hazel Marie Weatherman, Margaret and Douglas Archer, Fred Bickenheuser, and Russell and Kitty Umbraco.

We also highly recommend that you interact with other stretch glass collectors. The Stretch Glass Society was established in 1974 and its membership is dedicated to sharing information on stretch glass. This society meets once a year and fellow collectors gather to show interesting pieces and trade glassware. If you are interested in learning more about stretch glass, write to:

Stretch Glass Society
P.O. Box 573
Hampshire, IL 60140

We would like to thank all the collectors who shared their collections so that we could photograph and illustrate examples named within these book covers. Though we are bound to leave out some important contributors, we wish to thank:

Roy Ash
Mildred & Wesley Bicksler
Jean & Tom Bucher
Suzanne Burke
Debra & Bill Cotter
William Crowl
Lavina & John Decker
Judy & Paul Douglas
Frank M. Fenton & The Fenton Art Glass Co.
David Goodrich
Calvin Hackeman
Carol & Michael Jasman
Annette & David Jenkins
Helen & Bob Jones
Augusta Keith
John Madeley
Doris & Bill Mahan
Joyce & David Middleton
Paul Miller
Sharon & Ken Pakula

Tina Pendola
Janet Reichling
Joanne Rodgers
Rosa Schleede (deceased)
Ramona & Eldon Schroeder
Sharon Seglar
Renée & Dave Shetlar
Arna & Fred Simpson
Pam & Jim Steinbach
Thomas Steinle (deceased)
Rex Tatum
George Thomas
Kitty & Russell Umbraco
Karma Vullo
Nora Whitworth
Berry Wiggins
Photos: John Madeley
Photographic Reproductions: Martina Horn
Text: David Shetlar
Editing: Janet Reichling & Renée Shetlar

Preface

The authors, John Madeley and David Shetlar, have been collecting stretch glass for a couple of decades. Over this period of time, they realized that many glass dealers and collectors may have been able to identify an iridescent piece of glass as stretch glass, but most have little appreciation of the diversity of stretch glass. Many have no idea of the manufacturers and the true names associated with this elegant glass. Though several books have been published on general lines of glassware produced by major glass factories (e.g., Diamond, Fenton, Imperial, and Northwood), none of these books has illustrated the full range of stretch glass that was produced.

John Madeley is an engineer associated with a manufacturing firm in the Chicago area. As with many glass collectors, he has other collection passions, especially items related to the NASCAR racing circuit. He also collects other elegant glassware made in the 1920s and 1930s. John is vice president of the Stretch Glass Society.

David Shetlar is an associate professor of landscape entomology with The Ohio State University. He collects antique insect control devices and old woodworking tools. Dave and his wife, Renée, serve as co-presidents of the Stretch Glass Society.

It is expected that this book will answer many questions about the identity of both common and uncommon pieces of stretch glass that are already in the hands of collectors and that may come on the market in the future. However, with the presentation of this information, other unidentified or unusually colored and decorated pieces will surface.

The authors are extremely interested in learning about any unillustrated and unusual pieces of stretch glass not in this book. As time goes on, this book will be revised and the authors would certainly like to include any new pieces that have been found.

For this reason, the authors have a post office box through which you can correspond and send requests for identification or additional information. However, the authors are NOT IN THE BUSINESS OF PROVIDING APPRAISALS! If you have a piece of stretch glass not illustrated in this book or you need help in identifying a piece, please send a clear picture with measurements. If you need the picture back, please enclose a SASE.

All correspondence can be sent to:

John Madeley and David Shetlar
P.O. Box 901
Hampshire, IL 60140

(Note: this address is not that of the Stretch Glass Society.)

Be sure to include a return address, phone number, and e-mail address (if available).

Stretch Glass Defined

What is Stretch Glass?

Stretch glass collectors are often amused by the reaction of antique dealers when told that we are looking for "stretch glass." Some figure that we must be talking about the soda bottles that were stretched out of proportion in the 1960s. Most simply shrug their shoulders and ask that we point out a piece if we find one in the store. Because of its iridescence, stretch glass is often thought to be some kind of "art glass" or some kind of "strange carnival glass." In fact, stretch glass was described as the "poor man's" Tiffany or Steuben art glass when it was presented to the glass distributors in 1917 (February 8, 1917, Pottery, Glass and Brass Salesman).

We have also seen several pieces with "LCT" scratched into the bottom and even an acid etched, faked Steuben fleur-de-lis trade mark has surfaced. In every case, these pieces of glass have the heavier feel of true stretch glass, the mold marks, and occasionally, ground maries (a small holding rim that is later ground off) that are often mistaken for pontils.

To add to the confusion, several carnival authors refer to stretch glass as "stretch carnival." Early carnival was considered defective if the iridescence exhibited stretch marks! However, several of the later pieces, especially some made by Imperial, had the stretch effect applied.

We like the official definition of the Stretch Glass Society. They define stretch glass in their constitution and by-laws as follows: "Stretch Glass is pressed or blown-molded glass that has little or no pattern and is sprayed with a metallic salt mix while hot. When finished, this handmade glass will have either a cobweb iridescence (equal to stretch marks) or a plain iridescence effect, and is velvet or shiny in luster. In some rare instances, some stretch glass with an all-over pattern will have been put in the manufacturer's line of stretch. Old Stretch Glass was made in the United States from circa 1916 thru 1935."

Though stretch glass is commonly called "mass produced" or "machine made" glass, these terms do not realistically portray the process by which stretch glass is made. Though a mold is used to give the glass its basic shape, stretch glass has to be heated enough to bind the metallic salt to the glass surface, reheated to achieve the stretch effect, and reshaped to produce a maximum stretch effect.

Making of Stretch Glass

Carnival glass generally has obvious impressed designs — fruits, plants, animals, or pressed-cut designs. Stretch glass may have regular plain panels, rays, or rings but is generally devoid of elaborate designs. However, the main difference between stretch glass and carnival glass is the application of the iridescence-forming metallic salt spray during the making of the piece.

In carnival glass production, the glass is molded and shaped before the spray is applied. This results in a shiny surface, though a heavy spray or several sprayings may result in a matt or velvet finish. Stretch glass is sprayed when the glass is hot but after spraying, the piece is reheated and often reshaped to produce the characteristic stretch marks.

The stretch marks are caused by the difference in expansion rate of the underlying glass and the surface glass that has been bound to the metallic salt. Simple reheating produces a velvet surface with fine stretch marks. In order to make the stretch marks more dramatic, further shaping of the piece is needed. In short, stretch glass is reheated and usually reshaped after the iridescence is applied.

Obviously, the iridescent stretch effect can be added to both pressed or blown-molded glass as well as hand-made art glass. Occasionally, one will find some carnival glass with the stretch effect. Though there are some indications that this was a "mistake" and most carnival glass with this effect was destroyed, there are certain pieces where the stretch effect must have been deliberate. Stretch glass purists do not like their glass "cluttered" with fruits, flowers, animals, or insects and consider only simple lines or uniform patterns as acceptable for "true" stretch glass. We simply believe that beauty is in the eye of the beholder. We also cherish the glass that was made which appear to be "cross over" pieces in the manufacturer's attempts to produce new and different items.

Much of the true art glass has iridescence and stretch effects which cause considerable confusion among collectors and dealers. Most of the shiny to satin iridescence in Durand, Steuben, and Tiffany art glass is due to chemicals mixed in the glass. Additional iridescence with stretch effect may have been from metallic salts sprayed on the piece and enhanced with shaping. True art glass will generally have a pontil mark on the base which may be ground and polished or rough. Art glass from the same period as true stretch glass is usually quite thin and delicate. Recent art glass pieces may have the same weight as stretch glass, but no mold marks should be visible.

Unfortunately, several pieces of true stretch glass had a basal knob, called the "marie," formed in the mold. This knob was used to grasp the glass for handling during iridizing and shaping. After finishing, this marie was ground off and polished. To the inexperienced eye, this looks exactly like a polished pontil! To add to the confusion, unscrupulous individuals have even signed or applied art glass company insignias to these "ground marie" pieces.

One of the best ways to differentiate a ground marie from a ground pontil is to scrape your finger nail across the rim of the ground spot. If your finger nail feels a slight rim or lip along the edge, then it is probably a ground marie. If no rim is felt, it is probably a ground pontil. As far as we currently know, there are no rough finished maries. Therefore, a rough pontil indicate art glass of some sort.

Many stretch glass plates and some bowls have a ground "foot" or basal rim, also called the marie by glass workers. Again, inexperienced collectors often wonder if this is art glass or simply a piece of glass recently ground down because of chips or breaks. Neither case is true. These are simply pieces which were "stuck up" during their manufacture. In these pieces, instead of having a small marie which is ground off or a large marie (the normal molded "foot") which is grasped with a special tool called a "snap," the flat bottom was heat-attached to a metal, flat-ended rod for spraying and shaping. After shaping, the rod was tapped and the piece of glass was detached. This left a rough rim which was subsequently ground smooth on a large polishing wheel. It is common to have small glass flakes or some roughness found on these "stuck up" rims.

Many companies added enamel paint designs, stencils, gold paints and trims, or gold painted etched designs to the rims of their stretch glass. Some companies added wheel engraved designs that cut through the iridescence to their plates, bowls, and vases. Apparently, many of the manufacturers sold stretch glass "blanks" to other finishing companies. These companies then added painted designs, etched rims or even attached silver plated rims and bases to the pieces.

At the end of the iridescent glass manufacturing period, many of the glass companies applied an overall enamel paint to the outer surface of the glass. The Lancaster Glass Company and the United States Glass Company made several lines whereby clear, or crystal, glass was iridized, stretched, and then enameled.

Stretch glass often has bubbles, pieces of refractory brick, handling marks, and cut-off tails. While not necessarily desirable in outstanding pieces, these inclusions and marks are evidence of the style of manufacturing. Bubbles occur in the "pot" or holding tank for the molten glass and during the taking of a "gather" from the pot. If the molten glass gather is rotated too rapidly or slowly, air bubbles are trapped in the glass before a piece is cut off into the mold. If these bubbles are close to the surface of the finished piece, they may break out when cleaned or if handled roughly.

Many pieces of stretch glass will have tiny, white to cream colored pieces encased within the glass. These pieces are usually tiny flakes of refractory brick which line the holding tanks. Again, if these flakes are completely enclosed within glass they rarely cause problems. However, several collectors have stated that glass containing these inclusions may break or chip out, especially if subjected to rapidly changing temperatures.

1. Taking a gather from the pot. A metal rod is rotated into the molten glass (the "hot metal") until the correct amount of glass is gathered. This is quickly moved to the mold and press area.

Stretch glass is commonly "snapped up" or held with metal rods tipped with round clamps on the ends (the "snap"). If these snaps are not properly coated with lime, the snaps may leave some dark markings on the foot. Likewise, when the glass is shaped with metal crimps or wooden paddles the pieces may get some surface irregularities or markings. Finished pieces are often held on a metal fork while being carried to the lehr and this fork may make marks or leave iron flakes on the sides or feet of pieces. Again, these imperfections are not desirable but are simply the result of the manufacturing process.

Many bowls and other open pieces appear to have an irregular line or expanded, C-shaped crack on the surface. This is merely the "tail" that results when the molten glob of glass is cut off the gather rod to drop into the mold. The shear cools the glass at this spot, and the cooler area leaves an impression in the surface of the finished piece.

2. Cutting off the gather. The molten glass is allowed to drip into the mold. The press operator visually determines when enough glass has entered the mold and then cuts the mass from the gather. Where the glass was cut, it cools. This often leaves a "cutoff mark" in the final product. These cutoff marks can be on the inside or outside of a piece, depending on the type of mold used.

3. The assembled mold loaded with molten glass is placed under the plunger.

4. The plunger is lowered. This forces the molten glass into all the areas of the mold and up to the top ring of the mold.

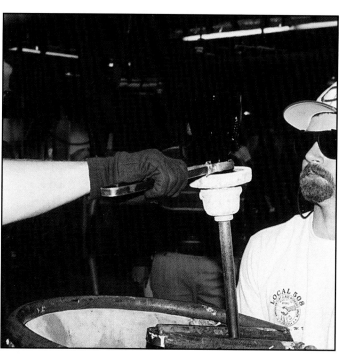

5. The mold is opened and the molded glass piece is removed. In this case the twin dolphin piece has the base cooled so that it will remain upright when further handled.

6. The molded piece is taken over to a snap. This is a metal rod with a round clamp on one end. This metal clamp exactly fits the foot of the piece. The snap is coated with lime to keep the hot glass from sticking to the metal. The snap is opened and closed by pressing the other end on the floor.

7. A "snapped up" piece ready to be reheated and finished.

8. The snapped up glass is placed inside a "glory hole." This is a blast furnace with ports to reheat the glassware.

9. After reheating, the snapped up piece is placed into a spray booth and the metallic salt spray, the "dope," is applied. The water immediately vaporizes, leaving an iridescent forming film of metal.

10. The doped piece is reheated and the magic of stretch glass occurs. The glass expands at a greater rate than the area where the dope was applied. This causes the checks and crackles characteristic of stretch glass.

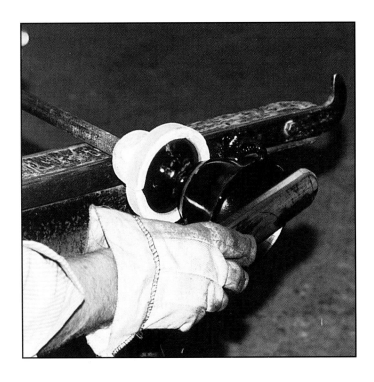

11. Further shaping of the doped and reheated piece emphasizes the stretch marks.

12. Placing the pieces into the lehr. Heating and shaping of the glass causes considerable internal stress. If the glass cools too rapidly, this internal stress can cause the piece to shatter. The lehr is a heated oven with a conveyer belt. Over several hours, the piece is allowed to cool very slowly. This releases most of the stress and reduces the chances of the glass shattering.

Stretch Glass Manufacturers

Many American glass companies made iridized glass of some sort shortly after the beginning of the twentieth century. Many of the companies made only a carnival type of glass or they may have applied a light, shiny iridescence to make a "pearl" effect. Neither of these types of iridized glass fits the definition of true stretch glass and these lines are not covered herein. However, we would not be surprised if a single piece or two of glass made by one of these companies turned up with a stretch effect. In fact, we know of a piece or two of iridized glass made by the Consolidated Glass Company which were given a stretch iridescent finish. Again, these appear to have been experimental pieces and were not produced or marketed in any great quantity.

As of the writing of this book, we are aware of nine principal manufacturers of what we would recognize as stretch glass. They are:

Central Glass Works of Wheeling, West Virginia
Diamond Glass-Ware Company of Indiana,
    Pennsylvania
Fenton Art Glass Company of Williamstown,
    West Virginia
Imperial Glass Company of Bellaire, Ohio
Jeannette Glass Company of Jeannette, Pennsylvania
Lancaster Glass Company of Lancaster, Ohio
H. Northwood & Company of Wheeling, West Virginia
United States Glass (probably Factory K, King Glass
    Company, Pittsburgh, Pennsylvania) and Tiffin
    Glass Company (Factory R, Tiffin, Ohio)
Vineland Flint Glass Works of Vineland, New Jersey

We have no doubt that all of these companies made significant amounts of stretch glass though some of the companies, like Vineland Flint Glass Works, left very little in the way of information as to their line names, colors, or even item or mold numbers.

There is also some confusion about the United States Glass Company. This company was established to combine several glass manufacturing plants across the country so that molds could be shared and different plants could specialize in the making of certain glass types. Included in this consortium was Tiffin Glass Company, Tiffin, Ohio (designated as Factory R). There are several advertising plates which have "Aurora" effect (the U.S. Glass name for the stretch glass effect) listed along with the Tiffin Glass logo. Some feel that this logo was placed on several of the U.S. Glass advertising plates since "Tiffin" was part of the U.S. Glass trademarks. More recent information indicates that many of the conglomerate companies were closed or sold and the Tiffin Factory became the "flagship factory" (Piña and Gallagher, Tiffin Glass 1914 – 1940). The "USGC" logo was altered in 1927 to have a large "T," and the Tiffin catalogs contained glassware produced in other plants. Therefore, presence of the logo does not imply that the glass was actually manufactured in the Tiffin, Ohio, plant. We would not be surprised to learn that both the King Glass Company and the Tiffin Glass Company iridized and stretched glass and may have even used the same molds! Until archeological evidence (digs that yield glass shards with stretch effects) or other written documentation is discovered, we may never be able to resolve these dilemmas.

Collecting Stretch Glass

Acquiring Stretch Glass and Determining Values

Stretch glass was distributed by the manufacturers and their marketing agents across all of the United States. Collectors, antique dealers, and home owners have further distributed stretch glass through their commerce and movement. While some areas of the country may have more stretch glass than others, we have never found a region of the country completely devoid of stretch glass. As with most collectibles, check out local flea markets, antique shows, antique shops, auctions, and even garage sales.

Many beginning collectors fell in love with a certain color, such as the more common blues, topaz (yellow or vaseline), greens and pinks. Their "search image" is often restricted to this one color and they may pass up other interesting pieces, simply because they don't recognize them as stretch glass. Many of the rare opaques are commonly missed because one is looking for blue, topaz, green or pink! Likewise, the darker purples and reds can be passed up if they are hidden in dark corners of a dealer's booth.

Unfortunately, stretch glass is like other collectibles that vary considerably in color, shape, and iridescence due to the manufacturing process. Most stretch glass collectors like strong iridescence and highly evident stretch marks. However, some pieces do not lend themselves to expression of these stretch marks. Candy jar lids, candlesticks, and similar pieces which have little or no reshaping after the iridescence is sprayed will have a shiny, satin to velvet finish. In these pieces, this is all one can expect.

Certain colors have always seemed to attract attention. Red stretch was probably produced in greater quantity than its availability would suggest. However, since it is a highly desired color, it commands greater prices. Jade Green (opaque green) and Mandarin Yellow (opaque yellow) are probably less common than red stretch, but collectors generally do not like these colors or iridescence as well. In addition, because of the scarcity and desirability of red carnival, red stretch is often picked up by carnival collectors.

Damaged stretch glass should be passed up unless it can be acquired for a small fraction of its worth when perfect. Carefully inspect the upper rim of stretch glass since heavy stretching can actually look like flakes broken from the rim. If in doubt, look at the suspect spot with a 10 to 15 power hand lens. Likewise, carefully inspect upper rims that may have been ground down where a flake was broken out. Antique shows and malls often have a glass repair business that can cover up damage too well for the unsuspecting consumer to detect.

Other common types of damage include cracks, handle separation, and "bull's-eye" marks. To detect these types of damage, hold the piece up to a strong light and rotate it at all angles. True cracks will show up as a shiny imperfection passing completely through the glass. Some stretch glass may have surface checks, due to the molding process or heavy application of iridescence which can look like cracks. However, when held in strong light, these will not appear as going totally through the glass. Handles of pitchers commonly separate or even break off. These may have been reglued so that the damage is barely detectable. Again, hold the area in front of a strong light. The bull's-eye marks are caused when something heavy strikes the glass. They are most commonly found in the bottoms of bowls and vases. Again, they can be detected easily with strong light. They will appear as small concentric rings or reflections.

In summary, determining a value for a piece of stretch glass must include: iridescence, stretch mark intensity, glass and iridescence color, rarity, and condition.

We highly recommend that you collect stretch glass because you enjoy "the hunt" or simply like the stretch glass colors and aesthetic appeal. Like most collectibles, don't expect to get rich by "investing" in stretch glass. If you like the piece and it fits your budget, why not indulge your collecting habit?

Handling and Cleaning Stretch Glass

Even though stretch glass is made by heat binding a metal salt to the glass surface, occasionally the binding is not strong enough to withstand vigorous cleaning, especially if an abrasive cleaner is used. The marigold-type (iron chloride salt spray) iridescence seems to be the most susceptible to this wear from cleaning.

Though each collector has his or her own "special technique" for cleaning glassware, we strongly recommend that simple dishwashing detergent and warm water be used with a soft washcloth before anything stronger is tried. Stretch glass may have been placed on a shelf in the kitchen and over the years accumulated a coating of airborne oil and dust. This grime can be difficult to remove without repeated applications of soapy water.

Self-adhesive price tags and tape tend to leave a sticky residue which defies normal washing. We have found that soaking the adhesive residue overnight in soapy water, or coating the tag residue with a sprayable oil (like WD-40™) for a few minutes will allow complete removal of the adhesive with soap and water.

Calcium and phosphorous scale, the white residue left behind when water evaporates in a container, is a bit more difficult to remove. Again, we suggest that you start with the weakest remover and work up. Fill the piece with common white vinegar (acetic acid) if the scale is on the inside. If the scale is on the foot of the piece (many bowls were placed in a larger bowl and both were filled with water and flowers for centerpieces), try to set the affected piece in a larger pan of vinegar. Let the piece sit for 24 hours before cleaning with soapy water. If this treatment does not remove the scale, a 50:50 solution of muriatic acid (hydrochloric) can be tried. Let the piece soak for a few minutes to a couple of hours only. To make the 50:50 solution, pour a cup or two of the concentrated muriatic acid into an equal amount of cool water. NEVER pour the water into the muriatic acid. Also, provide yourself with adequate ventilation since muriatic acid can release considerable amounts of chlorine gas. If neither of these treatments removes the scale, the damage is probably permanent.

Several of our fellow collectors use metal polishes, non-abrasive scouring powders, and even regular dishpan abrasives. We have seen too many pieces destroyed with these techniques. If we are to consider ourselves as merely temporary custodians of our precious stretch glass, we should make every effort to keep it from further damage.

Pieces which are covered with an exterior coating of enamel often have the enamel crazed or beginning to show some type of white roughness. We have found that, after simple cleaning, an application of common paste wax seems to cover up this crazing and slow its spread.

We also encourage collectors to keep painted, decalled, and gold rimmed pieces in the state that they were found. These applications often come off easily with mild abrasive soaps. Unfortunately, the decorations usually leave an impression in the surface iridescence which can not be removed.

Many pieces of stretch glass have been destroyed by poor packing and shipping. We highly recommend that pieces being shipped be completely separated from each other with foam or bubble wrap. These pieces should then be tightly packed with padding materials in the center of a spacious, crush resistant box. If you can feel the piece move when you shake the box, it isn't packed well and additional padding is essential. We've even been told that marking a package "FRAGILE" is interpreted as "toss underhanded!"

Disposing of Collections

No one likes to think about the inevitable end of a collecting effort — disposal of the collection. However, we strongly suggest that the conscientious collector should begin to think about what should be done with his or her collection. In recent years, many collections of all sorts have been donated to museums. Unfortunately, most museums are not well financed and many cannot handle these donations unless the collection is also endowed with maintenance funds. In fact, many of the conscientious museums will no longer accept a collection unless sufficient funds are provided for the collection's maintenance and display. Many museums are actually finding legal means of disposing of extensive collections which no longer can be maintained or no longer fit into the museum's area of interest.

We recommend that you may want to make a small donation of a piece or two of stretch glass to a museum which is interested in displaying American crafts, glassware, or manufactured goods. You could probably help the museum more by selling your collection on the open market or at auction and donating the monies realized from the sale than donating an extensive collection.

Your stretch glass collection should be considered part of your estate and, like all estates, planning is necessary if you have wishes as to what is to be done. We recommend that you become close friends with fellow stretch glass collectors and assign one or more of these friends as someone to be contacted by the executor of your estate. These friends should be knowledgeable enough to help the executor arrange for a proper sale or auction of the collection.

Stretch Glass Names and Colors

Names Used by Manufacturers

The name "stretch glass" was never used by the glass manufacturers nor contemporary distributors. As far as we can determine, this term was first used by the famous carnival and iridescent glass collector and book writer, Rose Presznick. The name was further formalized with the publication of stretch glass books by Berry Wiggins (1971) and Kitty and Russell Umbraco (1972).

The Fenton Art Glass Company and H. Northwood & Company were probably the two most important companies which had major impacts in introducing stretch glass to the glassware distributing industry. In many of the trade listings of 1917 to the mid-1920s, numerous references were made to what we call stretch glass today. The terms "iris," "cobweb iridescent," "crizzled," "lustre" (pronounced luss-tree), and "satin iridescent" were commonly used to refer to various iridescent glasses (carnival, stretch, and pearl).

Heacock, Measell and Wiggins (1991) mention that H. Northwood & Co. introduced their "Satin Sheen" line in mid-1916. This line was described in the July 20, 1916 issue of Crockery and Glass Journal as an "assortment of Tiffany finish glass." This line was further described in the February 8, 1917 issue of Pottery, Glass and Brass Salesman with the following statement:

"A brilliant new line of iridescent glassware called Satin Sheen, produced by the H. Northwood Company, is shown by C. J. Dela Croix at 19 Madison Avenue. The iridescence is brought out in an exquisite blue, purple and rarely beautiful pearl. The shapes are classic reproductions of old antiques in bowls, vases in wide variety, flared vases, lipped bowls and many other quaint effects."

Later, a circa 1920 Northwood advertising folder describes glassware called "Rainbow and Cobweb." The illustrated pieces are further described with: "All of the items shown here may be obtained in Blue Iris and Topaz Iris except the numbers 650 and 594. The following numbers can also be furnished in Blue Cobweb and Canary Cobweb..."

Fenton introduced their stretch glass in 1917 as "Silver Sun" (see Fenton Glass The First Twenty-five Years, page 135.) However, many of the 1921 advertising pieces refer to obvious stretch glass pieces as "Fenton Florentine."

The Diamond Glass-Ware Company's production of stretch glass is covered by Heacock, Measell and Wiggins (1993) where several trade publications are cited. In a June 9, 1921 Crockery and Glass Journal report, the following iridescent wares are cited: "The line of colored glassware turned out by the Diamond Glass-Ware Co... has been augmented by a number of new pieces... The colors — Harding Blue, amethyst and pearl in crackled and other artistic effects — have a rich iridescent finish which adds to their attractiveness. Among the new items are a jardiniere, candlestick, vases in reproductions of antique shapes, flower centers, etc. The complete line comprises comports, flower bowls, plates and other articles."

The term "crackled" along with the descriptions of the line items and shapes must be describing stretch glass items.

The Imperial Glass Company produced much of the highest quality stretch glass, especially in their "Imperial Art Glass" line. This line is commonly referred to as "Imperial Jewels" by collectors though this name was never used by the manufacturer. This line consists of specific pieces which were listed and illustrated in the Imperial Glass Encyclopedia Volume 1 (Measell, 1995). However, other pieces of stretch glass appear in the many Imperial advertisements, as published by Margaret and Douglas Archer (1978), where the terms "ice," "crizzled satin," "satin iridescent," and "bright iridescent" were used as descriptives.

The United States Glass Company (including King Glass and Tiffin Glass) has existing advertisement pages which refer to "Aurora" and obviously illustrate stretch glass pieces. This term is also listed on other pages as an available effect.

The names used by Central, Jeannette, Lancaster and Vineland are much less known and future research may yield the names used to refer to their stretch glass.

Glass and Iridescence Colors

Many of the glass manufacturers used simple names such as crystal, green, blue and topaz or canary (yellow glass or what is commonly called "vaseline" today) for the colors of their glassware at the end of the 1800s. These rather generic color names were replaced with different, and probably more marketable names, when iridescent glassware was produced.

Though we prefer to use the actual names that each manufacturer used to identify their lines and colors, this causes considerable confusion. In each manufacturer's section, we will present detailed information on the lines and color names used. In this section, we will attempt to provide as many of the color names used by manufacturers as are currently known to us. We will also use generic color terms to describe the numerous colors known to us. We have attempted to limit the number of colors defined because we know that blue, green, and topaz glass can vary slightly from batch to batch. To try to provide definite names for each of the minor variations would be foolhardy and complicate matters more than necessary.

We also want to acknowledge the tremendous work done by Berry Wiggins to locate the names used by stretch glass manufacturers. His listing of stretch glass lines and colors has appeared in the Stretch Glass Society Newsletters.

The following general color listing and the color codes are used in the rest of this book to identify pieces of stretch glass. Unique color names, where known, have been conserved. (NOTE: capitalized color names are the documented names used by the original manufacturers.)

Definitions of Stretch Glass Colors and Names

amber — transparent, light yellow-orange/yellow-brown glass (e.g., Imperial's Amber Ice, not Northwood's Russet); (known to have been made by Fenton, Imperial, U.S. Glass, and Vineland) (Plates 292, 406, 661 & 755).

AQUAMARINE — transparent, very light blue-green glass (Fenton) (Plates 136 & 350).

black amethyst — almost opaque, extremely dark purple glass (Imperial and U.S. Glass) (Plate 698).

blue-green — transparent, dark blue-green or teal glass (Imperial's Green Ice only, not carnival glass's ice green) (Plates 359 & 385).

blue — transparent, medium blue glass (e.g., Fenton's Celeste Blue); (made by Central, Diamond, Fenton, Northwood, U.S. Glass, and Vineland) (Plates 24, 109, 521, 639 & 751). Northwood made a fair amount of a similar blue glass but in a darker hue (dark blue) (Plate 511).

black opaque — nearly opaque, black glass (e.g., Diamond's Egyptian Lustre); (made only by Diamond) (Plate 48).

blue smoke — transparent, clear glass with blue-gray iridescence (Imperial's Blue Ice only); often called just smoke (Plate 396).

blue smoke milk — opaque milk glass with blue-gray iridescence (Imperial only); often called just smoke on milk (Plate 381).

caramel slag — opaque, cream with dark brown streaks, slag glass (Vineland only); sometimes called caramel (Plate 765).

cobalt blue — transparent, dark blue glass (e.g., Fen-

ton's Royal Blue); made by Diamond, Fenton, and Vineland (Plates 21, 198 & 767).

CORAL — opaque, pink-yellow to orange-yellow slag glass (U.S. Glass only); often called salmon (Plate 700).

crystal — transparent, clear glass with white iridescence (e.g., Fenton's Persian Pearl); commonly called White; (made by Diamond, Fenton, Imperial, Jeannette, Lancaster, Northwood, U.S. Glass, and Vineland) (Plates 20, 107, 358, 491, 673 & 748).

custard — opaque, white-yellow glass (Northwood's Ivory only) (Plate 530).

green lustre — transparent, clear glass with green to yellow enameled under-side (Lancaster only) (Plate 501). See Ruby Lustre.

green — transparent, medium green glass (e.g., Fenton's Florentine Green) (made by Central, Diamond, Fenton, Jeannette, U.S. Glass, and Vineland) (Plates 1, 18, 102, 481, & 676).

dark green — transparent, dark green glass, often called emerald green; (Imperial and Northwood) (Plates 456 & 514).

JADE BLUE — opaque, light blue-green glass (Northwood only); often called opaque blue (Plate 508).

JADE GREEN — translucent, jade-green glass (U.S. Glass only); often called opaque green (Plate 690).

MANDARIN YELLOW — translucent, yellow glass (U.S. Glass only); often called opaque yellow (Plate 689).

marigold — transparent, clear glass with yellow-gold

iridescence (e.g. Fenton's Grecian Gold); (made by Diamond, Fenton, Imperial, Jeannette, Lancaster, and Northwood) (Plates 14, 271, 373, 477, 484 & 512).

marigold milk — opaque milk glass with heavy orange-gold iridescence (Imperial only) (Plate 380).

NILE GREEN — opaque, light with dark green streaks, slag glass (U.S. Glass only) (Plate 650).

OLD ROSE — translucent, light pink glass (U.S. Glass only); commonly called pink opaque (Plate 671).

olive green — transparent, green-yellow glass (a U.S. Glass unidentified color name though some Vineland Glass has similar color hues, not Northwood's Russet) (Plate 666).

opaque white — opaque, white glass with light iridescence (Northwood only) (Plate 542).

PEARL BLUE — opaque, light blue slag glass (U.S. Glass only) (Plate 643).

PEARL GRAY — opaque, cream with tan to dark brown streaks, slag glass (U.S. Glass only) (Plate 640).

PEARL GREEN — transparent, light green glass with green-gray iridescence (Imperial only); often called green smoke (Plate 374).

pink — transparent, pink glass (e.g., Fenton's Velva Rose); frequently has orange-brown cast, see Plate 225; (made by Diamond, Fenton, Imperial, Lancaster, U.S. Glass, and Vineland) (Plates 58, 144, 413, 504, 655 & 763).

purple — transparent, medium purple glass (e.g., Imperial's Pearl Amethyst); (made by Diamond, Imperial, Jeannette, Northwood, U.S. Glass, and Vineland) (Plates 7, 369 & 705).

dark purple — transparent, almost opaque purple glass (e.g., Diamond's Midnight Wisteria) (Plate 22).

light purple — transparent, light purple glass (e.g., Fenton's Wisteria); (made by Central, Diamond, Fenton, Imperial, U.S. Glass, and Vineland) (Plates 13, 106, 360 & 662).

purple-blue — transparent, purple-blue glass, possibly a light cobalt glass (made by U.S. Glass and Vineland) (Plate 684).

red — transparent, red-yellow to red-purple glass (e.g., Fenton's Ruby); (made by Diamond, Fenton, Imperial, and possibly U.S. Glass) (Plates 12, 105 & 389).

red slag — opaque, red slag glass (U.S. Glass only) (Plate 728).

ROSE ICE — transparent, clear glass with heavy red-orange-brown iridescence (Imperial and Lancaster); (Jeannette called this color Amber); often called a rich marigold or heavy marigold (Plate 487).

RUBY LUSTRE — transparent, clear glass with red enameled under-side (Lancaster only) (Plate 497).

RUSSET — transparent, green-brown-yellow glass (Northwood only) (Plate 506).

TANGERINE — transparent, yellow glass with orange iridescence (Fenton only) (Plate 108).

TOPAZ — transparent, yellow-green glass (often referred to as canary by glass companies and vaseline by collectors); (made by Central, Diamond, Fenton, Northwood, and U.S. Glass) (Plates 3, 15, 103, 523 & 653).

violet — transparent, cobalt blue-purple (Northwood's Royal Purple only) (Plates 563 & 627).

white lustre — transparent, clear glass with white enameled under-side (Lancaster only) (Plate 485). See Ruby Lustre.

Other Stretch Glass Effects
(Several Companies Enameled the Entire Under-Side of Pieces)

See Green Lustre — (Lancaster Glass only)
See Ruby Lustre — (Lancaster Glass only)
See White Lustre — (Lancaster Glass only)

CUMULA — crystal stretch with green and white enamel in cloud pattern (U.S. Glass only) (Plate 680).

POMONA — crystal stretch with leaf stencil enamel, entire piece with yellow (Plate 617) or red-purple (Plate 715) enamel (U.S. Glass only).

Key To Marks Used In Manufacturer Chapters

Names capitalized, e.g., Topaz, are names found in actual manufacturer advertisements or were referred to as manufacturer names in trade journals of the period. Color names not capitalized, e.g., marigold, are generic common names of colors.

Prices

We believe that one of the most difficult requests of authors of antique and collectible books is to price items discussed. Though we have traveled across the United States, there seems to be little consistency in the pricing of stretch glass. Unfortunately, many dealers do not know the origin and availability of the many stretch glass pieces and colors. Pieces are commonly labeled as being an "art glass" or a "different" carnival. We have tried to give an average price of the piece illustrated. Where the piece is a one-of-a-kind, we have asked the owner what price he or she would place on the item. These prices were occasionally "tempered" with our experience! The prices listed are for pieces in perfect condition and with good to above average iridescence. Any piece with damage, iridescence missing, or decoration removed should be dramatically reduced in value. Most experienced collectors will pick up damaged items only if they can serve as an example until a good example is found. **Where an especially rare color is illustrated, we have added a price listing of a more common piece.**

CENTRAL GLASS WORKS

Wheeling, West Virginia

Central Glass Works in Wheeling, West Virginia, produced stretch glass in the 1920s and on occasion used the name "2000 Line" when describing glass that can be interpreted as stretch glass. Trade journals also often used the term "Tiffani glass" when describing this line. Advertisements from the company state that six colors were available but only list the following four:

Topaz – possibly a marigold but most likely a bright yellow-gold (Plate 3).
Blue – a regular blue, like Fenton's Celeste Blue (not illustrated).
Purple – a wisteria or light purple (Plate 7).
Green – a regular green, like Fenton's Florentine Green (Plate 1).

To date, we have not seen what we would call a marigold in the common Central console sets. Though the topaz sets are fairly common, the blue glass pieces are the most common. Console sets of light purple and green are also known. Several sets of dark blue (actually a cobalt blue) candle holders are known though this color is not specifically described in the advertisements. Bowls are also known in a white or crystal stretch glass. Therefore, the other two colors known to us are:

cobalt blue – a dark blue like Fenton's Royal Blue (Plate 4).
crystal – crystal glass with light iridescence, like Fenton's Persian Pearl (not illustrated)

PLATE 1. Bowl, flared, Green,
9¾"w, 3¾"h, 3½"b, $45.00

PLATE 2. Bowl, flared rolled rim,
Green, 9¼"w, 3⅜"h, 3½"b, $45.00

PLATE 3. Bowl, flared, Topaz,
9⅝"w, 4"h, 3½"b, $65.00

PLATE 4. Candlesticks, cobalt blue,
7"h, 4"b, rare color, $150.00 pair

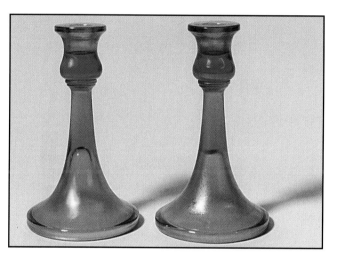

PLATE 5. Candlesticks, Green,
7"h, 4"b, $70.00 pair

PLATE 6. Candlesticks, Green,
9¼"h, 4⅜"b, $95.00 pair

PLATE 7. Console Set, Purple with "glue chip"
etching and gold decoration, rare color/decoration;
Bowl, flared, 10"w, 3½"h, 3½"b;
Candlesticks, 7"h, 4"b, $175.00 set

PLATE 8. Console Set, Green with "glue chip"
etching and gold decoration, rare decoration;
Bowl, rolled rim, 9"w, 3½"h, 3½"b;
Candlesticks, 7¼"h, 4"b, $150.00 set

DIAMOND GLASS-WARE COMPANY

Indiana, Pennsylvania

Diamond Glass-Ware Co., Indiana, Pennsylvania, produced stretch glass in the early 1920s and possibly late into that decade. The terms "Rainbow" and "Lustre" appear common in the trade journal descriptions and some occasional company advertisements. These are probably the line names. Advertisements and trade journal descriptions also have "crackled" and "shimmering" as descriptive terms. The term "crackled" may also refer to Diamond pieces which were blown into a mold which left irregular crackle glass-like marks on the exterior surface. These are fairly common in iridized and plain glass in blue and crystal. On the other hand, several rare, dark cobalt blue pieces are known that have heavy iridescence and a true crackle effect, possibly from application of so much metallic "dope" (see Plate 21). Numerous colors were described and there appear to be several names for the same colors, possibly simple marketing tools. The following colors are known to us:

Lustres –
    Egyptian Lustre – opaque black glass with multicolored iridescence (Plate 9).
    Golden Lustre – amber glass with golden-brown iridescence (not illustrated, none known).

Rainbow Lustres –
    Pearl – crystal glass with white iridescence (Plate 20).
    Gold – a marigold-like treatment (Plate 14).
    Blue – blue glass with light iridescence; like Harding Blue below (Plate 24).
    Green – green glass (Plate 10).
    Amethyst – purple glass (Plate 13).
    Royal Lustre – cobalt blue glass with silvery mirror iridescence not considered stretch (not illustrated).
    Ruby Lustre – ruby glass with silvery to gold mirror iridescence not considered stretch (not illustrated).
    Blue Crackle – cobalt blue glass with deep, multicolored iridescence (Plate 21).
    Harding Blue – normal blue glass, see Blue.
    Vesuvius Blue – no labeled example but this is assumed to be another common blue (not illustrated).
    After Glow – pink glass (Plate 58).
    Green Shimmering – green glass, see Green.
    Rose Shimmering – pink glass, see After Glow.
    Midnight Wisteria – a dark purple with multicolored iridescence (Plate 22).
    Twilight Wisteria – a medium purple, darker than the Amethyst but lighter than the Midnight Wisteria (Plate 27).
    red – a true ruby or red to amberina glass (Plate 12).

Some collectors include the Royal Lustre and Ruby Lustre in the stretch glass group because it was placed in the Lustre Line by Diamond. However, we have yet to find a piece with true stretch effects, and therefore, we do not include it as true stretch glass.

The most common Diamond stretch glass colors are green, blue, and crystal followed by purple, marigold, and pink pieces. Probably some of the most desirable colors are the Egyptian Lustre or black opaque stretch and the Blue Crackle or cobalt blue crackle stretch. Only a couple of red pieces are known.

PLATE 9. Bowl, cupped, Egyptian Lustre
(black opaque), 8¼"w, 4½"h", 3¾"b,
$125.00 ($40.00 b)

PLATE 10. Bowl, cupped, Green,
5¾"w, 2⅞"h, 3½"b, $35.00

PLATE 11. Bowl, cupped, Egyptian Lustre
(black opaque), 5⅝"w, 2⅝"h, 3⅜"b,
$95.00 ($40.00 b)

PLATE 12. Bowl, cupped, red,
8"w, 3¾"h, 4"b, $150.00

PLATE 13. Bowl, 3-mold, flared, Twilight
Wisteria/Amethyst (light purple),
7½"w, 2½"h, 2¾"b, $70.00

PLATE 14. Bowl, 3-mold, wide flared cupped,
Gold (marigold), 7⅛"w, 2¾"h, 2¾"b, $35.00

21

PLATE 15. Bowl, 3-mold, flared cupped, topaz, 6"w, 3"h, 2¾"b, $50.00

PLATE 16. Bowl, 3-mold, flared cupped, Twilight Wisteria/Amethyst (light purple), 6⅞"w, 3¼"h, 2¾"b, $70.00

PLATE 17. Bowl, 3-mold, flared cupped, red with gold etching, 6⅜"w, 3¾"h, 2¾"b, only one known, $175.00

PLATE 18. Bowl, flared straight side, Green, 10"w, 2¾"h, 4⅜"b, $35.00

PLATE 19. Bowl, wide flared cupped, Egyptian Lustre (opaque black), 7½"w, 1¾"h, 3½"b, $100.00

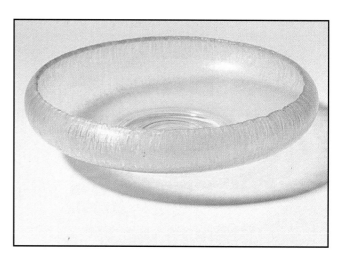

PLATE 20. Bowl, wide flared cupped, Pearl (crystal), 10¼"w, 2¾"h, 3⅞"b, scarce color, $80.00

PLATE 21. Bowl, wide flared cupped, Blue Crackle (cobalt blue crackle), 9½"w, 2¼"h, 4⅜"b, scarce color, $125.00

PLATE 22. Bowl, cupped, Midnight Wisteria (dark purple), 10¼"w, 2"h, 8⅝"b, scarce color/shape, $200.00

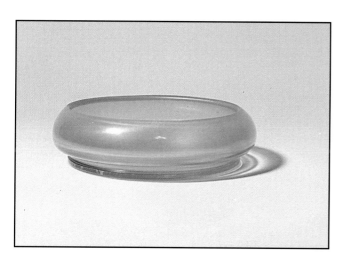

PLATE 23. Bowl, cupped, topaz, 8¼"w, 2¼"h, 7"b, scarce shape, $75.00

PLATE 24. Bowl, cupped, Blue/Harding Blue, 7"w, 1⅞"h, 5½"b, $45.00

PLATE 25. Bowl, crimped rim, dark green with marigold iridescence, 7½"w, 2¾"h, 5½"b, scarce color, $165.00

PLATE 26. Bowl, crimped rim, Blue/Harding Blue, 7½"w, 2⅞"h, 5½"b, scarce shape, $75.00

PLATE 27. Bowl, flared crimped rim,
Twilight Wisteria/Amethyst (light purple),
12¾"w, 2⅝"h, 8⅝"b, rare shape/color. $250.00

PLATE 28. Bowl, wide flared straight side,
Egyptian Lustre (black opaque),
9½"w, 2¼"h, 2⅞"b, scarce color, $135.00

PLATE 29. Bowl, 3-footed, cupped, Blue/Harding
Blue, 8"w, 2¼"h, scarce shape, $80.00

PLATE 30. Bowl, punch, flared straight side,
Blue/Harding Blue, 12"w, 6"h, 5"b, rare size,
$175.00

PLATE 31. Bowl, punch, cobalt blue,
15¾"w, 5¼"h, 6½"b, only one known, $1,000.00

PLATE 32. Bowl, rolled rim, Egyptian Lustre
(black opaque) with gold decoration,
9⅛"w, 2⅝"h, 3⅝"b, rare shape/color, $175.00

PLATE 33. Bowl, cupped "Rose Bowl," Green, 4⅞"w, 3¼"h, 2¼"b, $35.00

PLATE 34. Bowl, wide flared straight side on stand, Green, 10"w, 4⅛"h w/base, $65.00

PLATE 35. Comport, raised rim, "Adam's Rib," Blue/Harding Blue, 9½"w, 6⅜"h, 4¾"b, $75.00

PLATE 36. Comport, wide flared, "Adam's Rib," marigold milk, 11"w, 5½"h, 4¾"b, only one known, $2,000.00

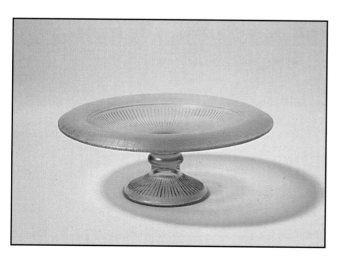

PLATE 37. Comport, rolled rim, "Adam's Rib," Green, 11¾"w, 4½"h, 4¾"b, $100.00

PLATE 38. Comport, hexagon foot, wide flared, Blue/Harding Blue, 9"w, 6¾"h, 4⅜"b, scarce shape, $95.00

PLATE 39. Comport, hexagon foot,
flared flattened, Green, 10½"w, 5¾"h, 4⅜"b,
scarce shape, $110.00

PLATE 40. Comport, sawtooth stem, raised rim,
Blue/Harding Blue, 6¼"w, 5⅜"h, 4"b, $45.00

PLATE 41. Comport, optic ray stem, raised rim,
Blue/Harding Blue, 6⅞"w, 5¼"h, 3¼"b, $60.00

PLATE 42. Comport, optic ray stem, two raised
sides, Gold (marigold), 7½"w, 6"h, 3¼"b, $55.00

PLATE 43. Comport, optic ray stem, three
raised sides, Green, 6½"w, 6"h, 3¼"b, $60.00

PLATE 44. Sherbet, smooth stem, Pearl (crystal),
3¾"w, 3⅜"h, 2⅝"b, scarce shape/color, $45.00

PLATE 45. Sherbet, ring on stem, Green,
3¾"w, 3⅜"h, 2⅝"b, $15.00

PLATE 46. Plate, two sets of rings, Blue/
Harding Blue, 5½"w, 1⅞"b, scarce shape, $25.00

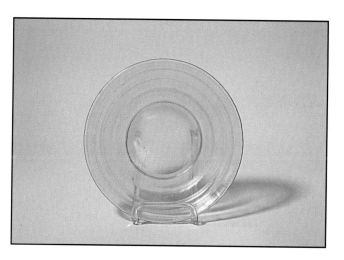

PLATE 47. Plate, two sets of rings, Green,
8⅞"w, 4¼"b, scarce shape, $60.00

PLATE 48. Plate, Egyptian Lustre (black opaque)
with gold decoration, 8⅜"w, 3½"b, scarce color,
$125.00

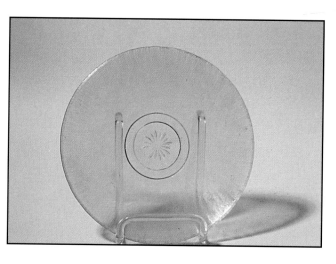

PLATE 49. Plate, pressed star base,
Green, 7⅝"w, 2⅝"b, $30.00

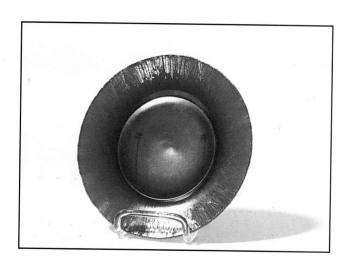

PLATE 50. Plate, ground marie, cobalt blue,
8¾"w, 5¼"b, rare color, $140.00 ($35.00 blue)

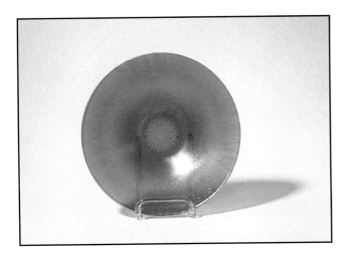

PLATE 51. Plate, pressed star base, Twilight Wisteria/Amethyst (light purple), 9⅞"w, 3⅛"b, scarce shape, $75.00

PLATE 52. Plate, Egyptian Lustre (black opaque), 11½"w, 5¾"b, scarce color, $150.00

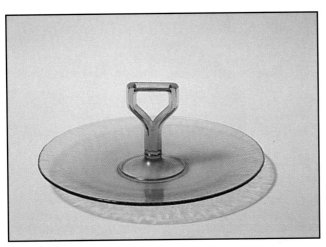

PLATE 53. Server, shovel handled, Green, 10¾"w, 4¼"h, 3⅜"b, $50.00

PLATE 54. Server, heart handled, Blue/Harding Blue, 10¼"w, 4"h, 3"b, $60.00

PLATE 55. Cheese and Cracker Set, Blue/Harding Blue, scarce shape; Cheese Dish, 5"w, 2¾"h, 3¼"b; Plate 10¾"w, 5¾"b, $90.00 set

PLATE 56. Bonbon, covered, Green, 5⅜"w, 5¾"h, 3½"b, $45.00

PLATE 57. Bonbon, covered, red,
5⅜"w, 6"h, 3½"b, one known, $800.00

PLATE 58. Candy Jar, covered, three footed,
After Glow (pink), 6⅜"w, 5¼"h, 2"b, rare shape,
$150.00

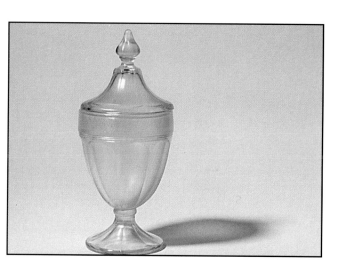

PLATE 59. Candy Jar, ¾-lb, Pearl (crystal),
3¼"w, 8⅛"h, 3"b, scarce color, $70.00

PLATE 60. Candy Jar, 1-lb, Blue/Harding Blue,
3⅞"w, 8¾"h, 3⅜"b, $60.00

PLATE 61. Candy Jar, covered, "Adam's Rib,"
Green, 3¾"w, 8⅜"h, 3¾"b, rare shape, $90.00

PLATE 62. Candlesticks, Blue/Harding Blue with
white enamel trim 9"h, 4⅜"b, $80.00 pair

PLATE 63. Candlesticks, Green,
8"h, 4¾"b, $80.00 pair

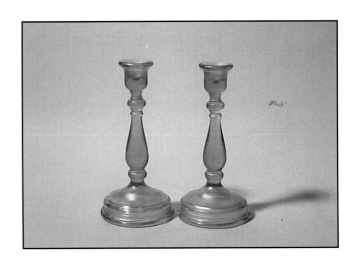

PLATE 64. Candlesticks, After Glow (pink,)
8¾"h, 2"b, scarce color, $125.00 pair

PLATE 65. Candlesticks, Blue/Harding Blue with
wheel cut decoration 8⅛"h, 5"b, unusual cutting,
$150.00 pair

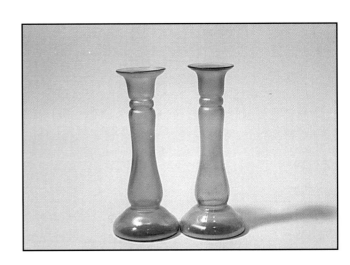

PLATE 66. Candlestick/Vase, Blue/Harding
Blue, 7¼"h, 3"b, $70.00 pair

PLATE 67. Candlestick/Vase, Blue/Harding Blue
with flower decoration, 9⅝"h, 2⅜"b, $90.00 pair
($60.00 w/o decoration)

PLATE 68. Candlestick/Vase, "Adam's Rib,"
Blue/Harding Blue, 7¾"h, 2¼"b, scarce shape,
$180.00 pair

PLATE 69. Candlestick/Bowl, "PAT APPLIED FOR" in base, Gold (marigold), 7⅜"w, 3"h, 4⅜"b, scarce color, $90.00

PLATE 70. Goblet, Green, 3⅛"w, 6½"h, 2⅝"b, scarce shape, $45.00

PLATE 71. Cup, punch, two sets of rings, Pearl (crystal), 3½"w, 2⅜"h, 1¾"b, rare shape, $55.00

PLATE 72. Cup, punch, crimped rim, two sets of rings, Blue/Harding Blue, 4"w, 2⅜"h, 1¾"b, rare shape, $70.00

PLATE 73. Mug, handled, Blue/Harding Blue with Souvenir 1925 decoration, 3⅜"w, 5"h, 2⅝"b, scarce shape/decoration, $125.00

PLATE 74. Mug, handled, "Adam's Rib," Blue/Harding Blue, 2¾"w, 5⅛"h, 2⅝"h, rare shape, $80.00

PLATE 75. Pitcher, "Adam's Rib," Blue/Harding Blue, 3"w, 9⅞"h, 3½"b, rare shape, $400.00

PLATE 76. Pitcher and Tumbler Set, Blue/Harding Blue, scarce shape; Pitcher, optic ribs, 4¼"w, 9"h, 4"b, $200.00; Tumblers, ribbed, 3"w, 4⅝"h, 2"b, $50.00 each

PLATE 77. Sugar, two-handled, "Adam's Rib," Green, 3½"w, 3⅞"h, 2¾"b, scarce shape, $50.00

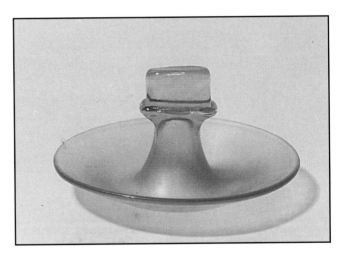

PLATE 78. Matchbox Holder, Green, 5¼"w, 1¾"h, 2⅜"b, rare shape, $150.00

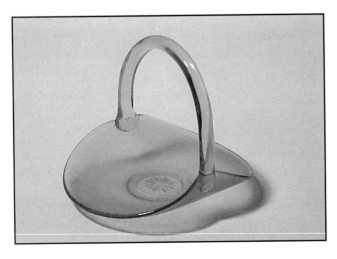

PLATE 79. Basket, pressed star base, Green, 7¾"w, 6¼"h, 2½"b, rare shape, $100.00

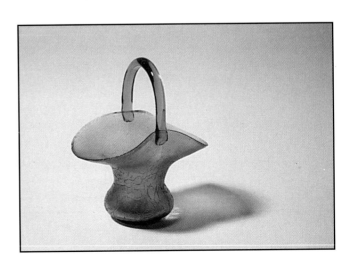

PLATE 80. Basket, crackle surface, Blue/Harding Blue, 8"w, 9½"h, 2¾"b, scarce shape/color, $100.00

PLATE 81. Vase, pinched, Blue/Harding Blue,
4"w, 4¼"h, 2⅛"b, $50.00

PLATE 82. Vase, Pearl (crystal),
4⅜"w, 4"h, 2¼"b, $50.00

PLATE 83. Vase, bulb shape, crackle surface,
Pearl (crystal), 3¾"w, 6½"h, 3¾"b,
scarce color, $90.00

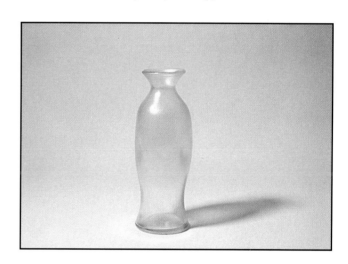

PLATE 84. Vase, pinched, Pearl (crystal),
2¾"w, 9¾"h, 3½"b, $90.00

PLATE 85. Vase, pinched, Green,
2½"w, 6"h, 2⅝"b, $55.00

PLATE 86. Vase, spittoon shape, Blue/Harding
Blue, 6½"w, 8½"h, 4¼"b, scarce shape, $125.00

PLATE 87. Vase, spittoon shape, Green,
6⅝"w, 5½"h, 2¾"b, $95.00

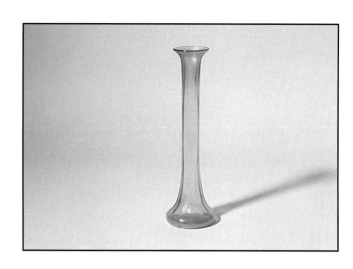

PLATE 88. Vase, ribbed, Green,
2"w, 8"h, 2⅝"b, $45.00

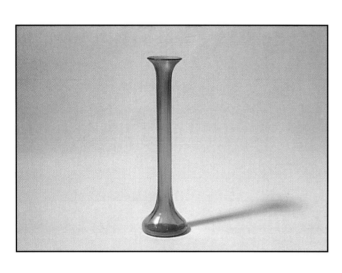

PLATE 89. Vase, ribbed, Blue/Harding Blue,
2⅜"w, 12"h, 3¼"b, $50.00

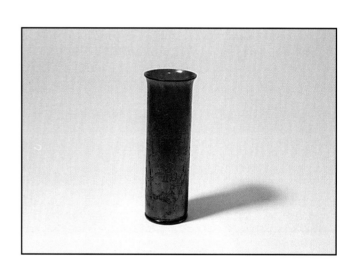

PLATE 90. Vase, Blue Crackle (cobalt blue),
3½"w, 9¾"h, 3"b, scarce color, $100.00

PLATE 91. Vase, Blue/Harding Blue,
5⅛"w, 11⅜"h, 5"b, $150.00

PLATE 92. Vase, "Adam's Rib," Blue/Harding
Blue, 4"w, 9¾"h, 3½"b, rare shape, $300.00

PLATE 93. Vase, fan, Green,
5¾"w, 8"h, 4"b, rare shape, $100.00

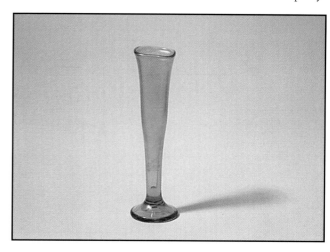

PLATE 94. Vase, bud, Blue/Harding Blue,
2⅝"w, 9¾"h, 2⅞"b, $35.00

PLATE 95. Vase, rolled rim, Egyptian Lustre
(black opaque), 4¾"w, 8⅝"h, 3⅝"b,
rare shape/color, $175.00

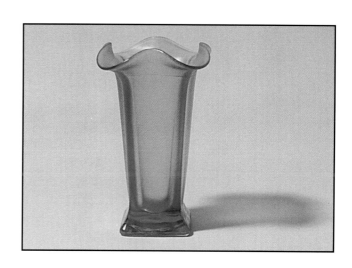

PLATE 96. Vase, square crimped top, Green,
4½"w, 6¼"h, 2½"b, $60.00

PLATE 97. Vase, flared, Blue/Harding Blue with
cutting, 6½"w, 8¼"h, 4"b, rare decoration,
$150.00

PLATE 98. Vase, flared top, Egyptian Lustre
(black opaque), 9⅜"w, 7⅛"h, 3⅞"b, rare color,
$300.00

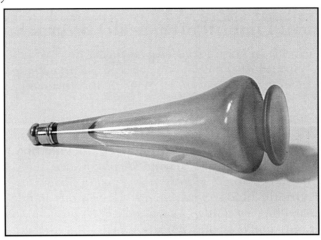

PLATE 99. Vase, car, Green with metal base,
2¼"w, 8¼"h, rare shape, $150.00

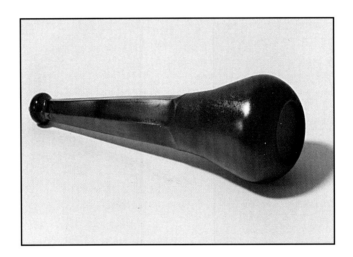

PLATE 100. Vase, car, cupped, marked Benzer,
(cobalt blue) 2⅜"w, 7⅜"h, rare color, $150.00

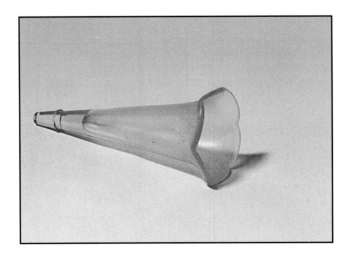

PLATE 101. Vase, car, crimped, Pearl (crystal),
2¾"w, 7⅛"h, $65.00

FENTON ART GLASS COMPANY

Williamstown, West Virginia

Fenton Art Glass Co., Williamstown, West Virginia, was one of the first companies to make stretch glass. They made this glass from 1917 through the early 1930s with most of the glass being made in the 1920s. This is the only original stretch glass manufacturer still in the glass manufacturing business today.

They made a line of 75th Anniversary pieces in stretch glass in 1982 and began making pieces regularly in traditional as well as new colors in the 1990s.

Though Fenton apparently used the term "Silver Sun" with the introduction of stretch glass in 1917, they eventually used the term "Florentine Ware" to refer to their stretch glass, and a number of color names were used. However, there are a couple of pieces which have been seen that are in colors which were probably not named.

Amber – a light to medium amber glass (Plate 292).
Aquamarine – a light blue-green glass, ice blue of carnival glass collectors (Plate 118).
Celeste Blue – blue glass (Plate 149).
Florentine Green – green glass (Plate 102).
Grecian Gold – clear glass with marigold iridescence (Plate 271).
Persian Pearl – clear glass with white iridescence (Plate 104).
Royal Blue – cobalt blue glass (Plate 198).
Ruby – red to amberina glass (Plate 105).
Tangerine – yellow glass with orange or marigold iridescence (Plate 108).
Topaz – a yellow-green glass, commonly called vaseline by general glass collectors (Plate 103).
Velva Rose – pink glass, though some pieces may have a salmon or brownish cast (Plate 226, pink & Plate 225, brownish).
Wisteria – light purple glass (Plate 106).

Fenton's Celeste Blue, Florentine Green, Grecian Gold, Persian Pearl, Topaz, and Velva Rose are all common colors though certain pieces may be rare to difficult to find in any of these colors. The Tangerine, Wisteria, Amber, and Aquamarine are less common though the Tangerine and Wisteria are generally more costly to acquire. The Royal Blue is probably the rarest color, followed by Ruby. Both are in high demand and they command premium prices. Generally, Fenton's Ruby bowls are not iridized on the outside surface.

The Grecian Gold is often difficult to differentiate from simple carnival marigold. Apparently Grecian Gold was sprayed twice and it usually has a satiny to slightly stretched finish while true marigold will be shiny overall.

PLATE 102. Bowl, #109, cupped, Florentine Green, 3¾"w, 2"h, 2½"b, $20.00

PLATE 103. Bowl, #545, cupped, Topaz, 5¼"w, 2"h, 2⅝"b, $45.00

PLATE 104. Bowl, #2005, mayonnaise, Persian Pearl (crystal), 5¼"w, 3⅛"h, 2⅜"b, $45.00

PLATE 105. Bowl, flared cupped, Ruby (red), 6"w, 3"h, 2"b, $90.00

PLATE 106. Console Set, Wisteria (light purple); Bowl, #607, shallow cupped, with oval cuts, 9½"w, 2⅝"h, 3¾"b, $150.00; Candlesticks, #349, with oval cuts, 10½"h, 4⅛"b, $300.00

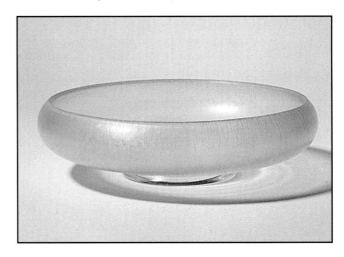

PLATE 107. Bowl, #607, wide flared cupped, Persian Pearl (crystal), 9¼"w, 2⅝"h, 3¾"b, $40.00

PLATE 108. Bowl, #647, wide flared, rolled rim,
Tangerine, 11½"w, 2⅛"h, 3½"b, $60.00

PLATE 109. Bowl, #604, aquarium, Celeste Blue
with black base, 9¾"w, 6"h, 4"b, $125.00

PLATE 110. Bowl, #846, flared-cupped, Tangerine with metal base, 8¾"w, 3⅛"h, 2⅞"b, $110.00

PLATE 111. Bowl, #647, flared, Celeste Blue
with decoration #2, 12¾"w, 2⅜"h, 3½"b, $110.00

PLATE 112. Bowl, #647, rolled rim,
Ruby (red), 10⅝"w, 3⅝"h, 3½"b, $150.00

PLATE 113. Bowl, #604, crimped rim,
Ruby (red), 11¼"w, 6¼"h, 4"b, $400.00

PLATE 114. Bowl, Punch Set, Florentine Green;
Bowl, #604, flared, 12"w, 5⅝"h, 4"b, $300.00;
Bowl Base, #604, 5"w, 5"h, 6½"b, $500.00;
Cup, punch, #604, 3⅛"w, 2⅜"h, 2"b, $40.00 each

PLATE 115. Bowl, #604, shallow cupped,
Persian Pearl (crystal) with black paint
decoration, 14¼"w, 2⅛"h, 4"b, $200.00

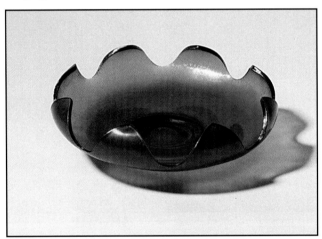

PLATE 116. Bowl, #848, wide cupped Tulip,
Wisteria (light purple), 8¾"w, 2¾"h, 3"b,
rare color, $150.00

PLATE 117. Bowl, #848, flared Tulip, Tangerine,
9"w, 3¼"h, 3"b, $80.00 ($60.00 blue)

PLATE 118. Bowl, #848, rose bowl Tulip,
Aquamarine, 6"w, 4"h, 3"b, scarce color, $90.00

PLATE 119. Bowl, #1522, double crimp,
Wisteria (light purple), 9¾"w, 3"h, 3⅜"b, $125.00

PLATE 120. Bowl, cupped, 5 rings, Tangerine, 6¾"w, 2¼"h, 2¾"b, $70.00

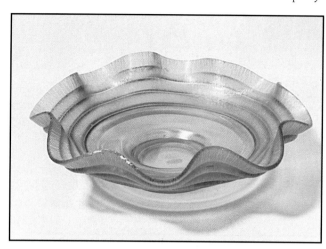

PLATE 121. Bowl, crimped, 5 rings, Celeste Blue, 7½"w, 2⅛"h, 2¾"b, $50.00

PLATE 122. Bowl, #1512, flared, ringed, Tangerine, 7¾"w, 4⅝"h, 3¾"b, $80.00

PLATE 123. Bowl, #1502, diamond optic, flared, Tangerine, 9⅝"w, 3¼"h, 4"b, $125.00

PLATE 124. Bowl, #1502, diamond optic, special rolled rim, Tangerine, 13"w, 3½"h, 4"b, $140.00

PLATE 125. Bowl, #638, flared cupped, 27 rays, Celeste Blue, 7¾"w, 1⅞"h, 3½"b, $35.00

PLATE 126. Bowl, #1502A, diamond optic, wide flared, three-dolphin, Florentine Green, 10"w, 2½"h, 2⅞"b, scarce shape, $160.00

PLATE 127. Bowl, #1504A, flared cupped, three-dolphin, Velva Rose (pink), 8¼"w, 3⅜"h, 2⅞"b, scarce shape/color, $120.00

PLATE 128. Bowl, #1504A, flared, three-dolphin, Aquamarine, 10"w, 2½"h, 2⅞"b, $125.00

PLATE 129. Bowl, #1504A, wide cupped, three-dolphin, Velva Rose (pink), 9½"w, 2¼"h, 2⅞"b, scarce shape, $120.00

PLATE 130. Bowl, #1504A, cupped, three-dolphin, Ruby (red), 6¾"w, 4"h, 2⅞"b, one known, $1,850.00

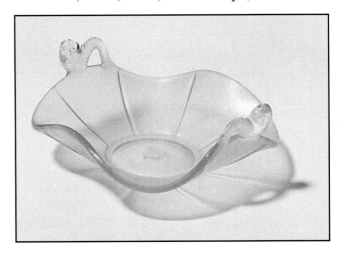

PLATE 131. Bowl, #1621, crimped, twin-dolphin, Florentine Green, 6⅜"w, 1½"h, 2½"b, scarce shape, $80.00

PLATE 132. Bowl & Under-Plate Set, Tangerine, rare shape/color; Bowl, Laurel Leaf rim, 10"w, 4¼"h, 3½"b, $150.00; Plate, Laurel Leaf rim, 13⅛"w, 3½"b, $150.00

PLATE 133. Bowl & Under-Plate Set, Celeste Blue, scarce shape; Bowl, #750, octagonal, ground foot, 9¼"w, 4¾"h, 4¾"b, $175.00; Plate, octagonal, ground foot, 11¾"w, 6¾"b, $75.00

PLATE 134. Bowl, #603, three-footed, wide-flared, Persian Pearl (crystal), 9½"w, 3⅛"h, 3⅞"b, $175.00

PLATE 135. Bowl, #603, three-footed, crimped, Ruby (red), 10⅜"w, 5¼"h, 2⅞"b, scarce color, $650.00

PLATE 136. Bowl, #349, ball footed, Aquamarine, ground marie, 9⅛"w, 3⅝"h, rare shape, $150.00

PLATE 137. Bowl, #250, footed, fern dish, flower decoration, Persian Pearl (crystal), 6½"w, 3⅜"h, 1⅛"b, scarce shape, $65.00

PLATE 138. Bowl, #312, footed, wide cupped, Celeste Blue, 6¾"w, 2"h, 3¼"b, $80.00

PLATE 139. Bowl, #231, footed, wide cupped, with ribs, Celeste Blue, 9¾"w, 3⅛"h, 5⅛"b, $80.00

PLATE 140. Bowl, #231, footed, cupped, with ribs, Celeste Blue, 7⅝"w, 4¼"h, 5⅛"b, $80.00

PLATE 141. Bowl, #847, flared, Melon-Rib, Persian Pearl (crystal), 8"w, 2½"h, 3¼"b, $40.00

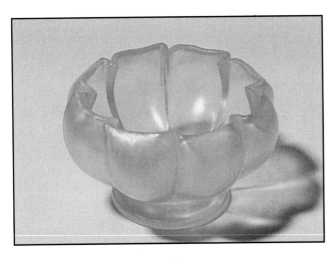

PLATE 142. Bowl, #847, cupped, Melon-Rib, Topaz, 5¾"w, 3⅜"h, 3¼"b, $60.00

PLATE 143. Bowl, #847, wide cupped, Melon-Rib, Wisteria (light purple), 7"w, 2½"h, 3¼"b, $85.00

PLATE 144. Bowl, #857, standard, Melon-Rib,
Velva Rose (pink), 7½"w, 5⅜"h, 4"b, $60.00

PLATE 145. Bowl, #857, cupped, Melon-Rib,
Tangerine, 7½"w, 5⅛"h, 4"b, $90.00

PLATE 146. Bowl, #857, flared cupped,
Melon-Rib, Tangerine, 9½"w, 4¼"h, 4"b, $100.00

PLATE 147. Bowl, #857, flared, Melon-Rib,
Tangerine, 11¼"w, 3½"h, 4"b, $100.00

PLATE 148. Bowl, #857, flared rolled,
Melon-Rib, Tangerine, 9¾"w, 3¾"h, 4"b, $100.00

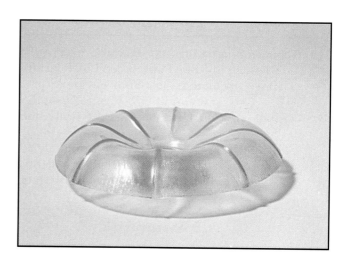

PLATE 149. Bowl, #857, special rolled rim,
Melon-Rib, Aquamarine, 11"w, 2⅜"h, 4"b, $90.00

PLATE 150. Bowl & Under-Plate Set, Persian
Pearl (crystal), scarce shape; Bowl, #1562-2-14,
Banana Boat, 14"w, 3¼"h, 5¾"b, $75.00;
Plate, #1562-3, flattened, 15¼"w, 5¾"b, $75.00

PLATE 151. Bowl, #1563, two-handled,
oval, Velva Rose (pink), 12¾"w, 4⅝"h, 6⅞"b,
scarce shape, $225.00

PLATE 152. Bowl, #550, 12-panel,
wide flared, Celeste Blue, 12¼"w, 4⅛"h, 4"b,
scarce shape, $120.00

PLATE 153. Bowl, #550, 12-panel, cupped,
Wisteria (light purple), 7⅜"w, 6½"h, 4"b,
rare shape/color, $350.00

PLATE 154. Bowl, #550, 12-panel, flared
cupped, Celeste Blue, 10¼"w, 5¼"h, 4"b,
scarce shape, $140.00

PLATE 155. Bowl, #550, 12-panel, rolled rim,
Velva Rose (pink), 11⅛"w, 3¾"h, 4"b,
scarce shape, $120.00

PLATE 156. Comport, #736, flared cupped,
rib optic, Florentine Green, 8"w, 4¼"h, 3¾"b,
$35.00

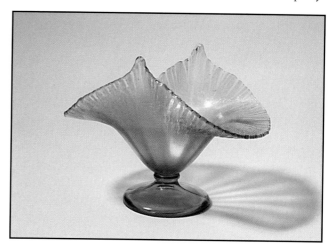

PLATE 157. Comport, #736, flared with sides
pulled up, Celeste Blue, 8⅝"w, 6½"h, 3¾"b,
$75.00

PLATE 158. Comport, #9, crimped,
Florentine Green, 7⅛"w, 4¾"h, 3½"b, rare shape,
$60.00

PLATE 159. Comport, #737, flared cupped,
Celeste Blue, 6¼"w, 4⅜"h, 3¾"b, $40.00

PLATE 160. Comport, #103, flared oval,
Celeste Blue, 4" x 4¾"w, 3"h, 2½"b, rare shape,
$75.00

PLATE 161. Comport, #923, flared oval,
Florentine Green, 6"w, 3¾"h, 3¾"b, $55.00

PLATE 162. Comport, #643, cupped,
Topaz, 5"w, 3¾"h, 3½"b, $40.00

PLATE 163. Comport, #1043, cupped,
Velva Rose (pink), 6"w, 3½"h, 3⅞"b, $60.00

PLATE 164. Comport, #712, cupped, Topaz,
6⅞"w, 3⅝"h, 3¼"b, scarce color, $75.00

PLATE 165. Comport, #1533A, twin-dolphin,
round, Topaz, 4¾"w, 4½"h, 3"b, $90.00

PLATE 166. Comport, #1533A, twin-dolphin,
flared, Tangerine, 6⅝"w, 4⅝"h, 3½"b, $125.00

PLATE 167. Comport, #1533A, twin-dolphin,
oval, Topaz, 6¾"w, 4"h, 3⅛"b, $100.00

PLATE 168. Comport, #1533A, twin-dolphin, square, Florentine Green, 6"w, 4½"h, 3"b, $100.00

PLATE 169. Comport, #1533A, twin-dolphin, square, Ruby (red), 7¼"w, 4¾"h, 3½"b, rare color, $1,200.00

PLATE 170. Comport, #1502A, twin-dolphin, diamond optic, flared, Tangerine, 5⅛"w, 5⅛"h, 3½"b, scarce shape, $125.00

PLATE 171. Comport, #1502A, twin-dolphin, diamond optic, square, Florentine Green, 6¾"w, 5⅛"h, 3½"b, scarce shape, $100.00

PLATE 172. Comport, #500, crimped, Ruby (red), 6½"w, 5¼"h, 2⅞"b, only one known, $350.00

PLATE 173. Comport, #260, wide flared, Tangerine, 6¾"w, 6⅛"h, 3¼"b, $90.00

PLATE 174. Comport, #260, flared,
Wisteria (light purple), 5⅞"w, 7"h, 3½"b,
scarce color, $125.00

PLATE 175. Comport, #1536, wide flared,
Velva Rose (pink), 6¾"w, 6¼"h, 3⅜"b,
scarce shape, $80.00

PLATE 176. Comport, #917, flared rolled rim,
Celeste Blue, 10¼"w, 4"h, 4⅛"b, scarce shape,
$125.00

PLATE 177. Comport, high-standard, flared,
Wisteria (light purple), 9⅝"w, 8⅛"h, 5"b,
rare shape/color, $250.00

PLATE 178. Comport, high-standard,
wide flared, Celeste blue, 11⅝"w, 7"h, 5"b,
scarce shape, $200.00

PLATE 179. Comport, #1608, twin-dolphin,
deep oval, Wisteria (light purple),
9⅞"w, 6½"h, 4⅛"b, scarce shape, $225.00

PLATE 180. Comport, #1604, twin-dolphin, oval, Florentine Green, 11"w, 5⅝"h, 4⅛"b, scarce shape, $110.00

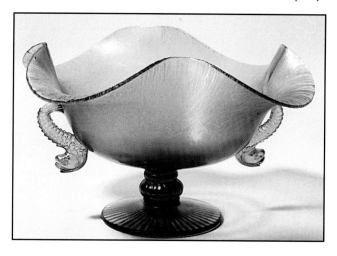

PLATE 181. Comport, #1602, twin-dolphin, square, Wisteria (light purple), 10½"w, 6"h, 4⅛"b, scarce shape, $200.00

PLATE 182. Comport, #1602, twin-dolphin, crimped, Aquamarine, 10¼"w, 5⅞"h, 4⅛"b, $175.00

PLATE 183. Salver, #643, Wisteria (light purple), 6½"w, 2⅝"h, 3½"b, $55.00

PLATE 184. Salver, #1043, Tangerine, 7¾"w, 2½"h, 3⅞"b, rare color, $90.00

PLATE 185. Salver, #1043, flared rolled rim, Velva Rose (pink), 7¾"w, 2½"h, 3⅞"b, $50.00

PLATE 186. Card Tray, #643, Celeste Blue,
7⅛"w, 2¼"h, 3½"b, $50.00

PLATE 187. Card Tray, #1502A, twin-dolphin,
diamond optic, Velva Rose (pink), 8"w, 2"h,
3⅜"b, scarce shape, $150.00

PLATE 188. Sherbet, #103, cobalt crest, Persian
Pearl (crystal), 4½"w, 3¼"h, 2½"b, rare
crest/color, $225.00 ($12.00 pink, $15.00 blue)

PLATE 189. Sherbet & Under-Plate Set, Florentine Green, $60.00 set; Sherbet, #403, 4½"w,
3¼"h, 2½"b, $35.00; Plate, #403, 8⅛"w, 4⅜"b,
$25.00

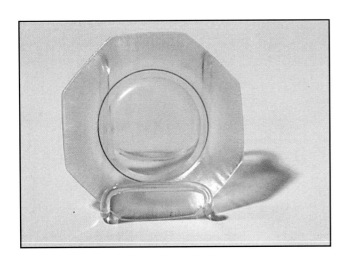

PLATE 190. Plate, #756, octagon,
Florentine Green, 6"w, 3⅜"b, $15.00

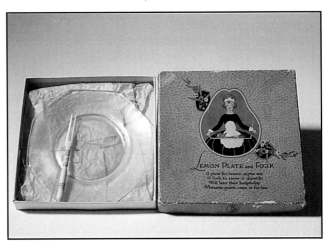

PLATE 191. Plate, #756, Lemon Server in
original box with fork, Topaz, 6"w, 3⅝"b,
$75.00 set

PLATE 192. Plate, #757, octagon, Laurel Leaf,
Celeste Blue, 7½"w, 4⅜"b, $35.00

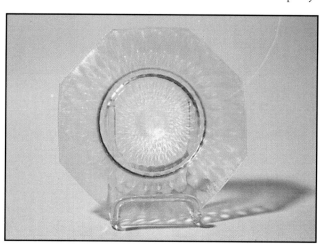

PLATE 193. Plate, #1502, diamond optic,
Velva Rose (pink), 7¾"w, 4¼"b,
scarce shape/color, $65.00

PLATE 194. Plate, #758, Wisteria (light purple),
8⅜"w, 6"b, $70.00

PLATE 195. Plate, #630, Wisteria (light purple),
ground marie, 8¾"w, 5¼"b, scarce color, $40.00

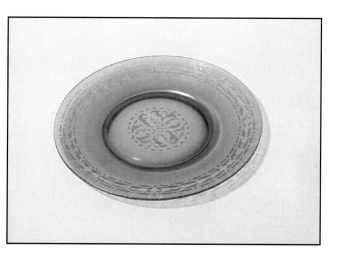

PLATE 196. Plate, #681, Wisteria (light purple),
with decoration #3, 8¼"w, 4⅜"b, rare etching,
$90.00

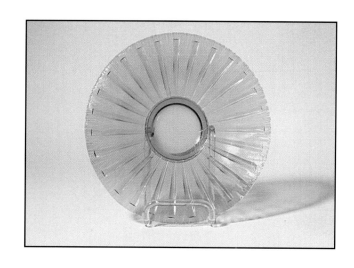

PLATE 197. Plate, #631, Celeste Blue,
9½"w, 3¾"b, $40.00

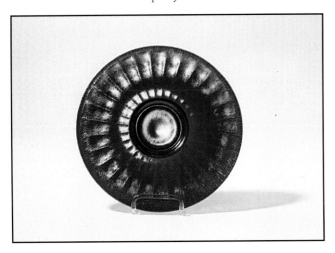

PLATE 198. Plate, #631, Royal Blue, cobalt blue, 11½"w, 3¾"b, $225.00 ($60.00 topaz)

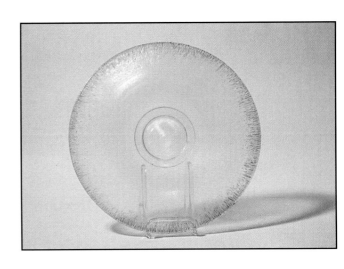

PLATE 199. Plate, #647, Florentine Green, 14"w, 3½"b, $60.00

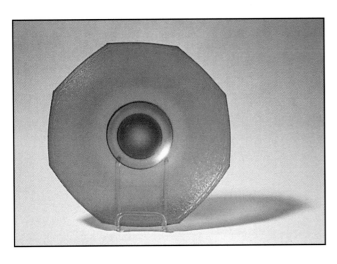

PLATE 200. Plate, octagonal, Laurel Leaf, Tangerine, 13⅛"w, 3½"b, $150.00

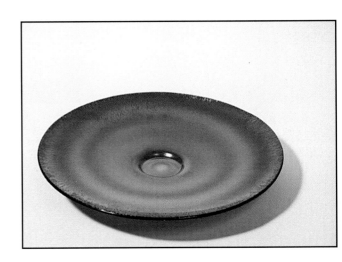

PLATE 201. Plate, #604, Ruby (red), 16¾"w, 4"b, $400.00

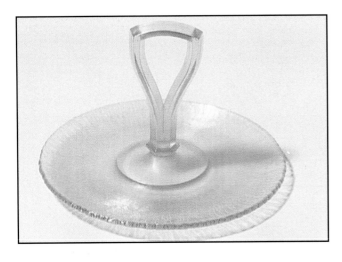

PLATE 202. Butter Ball Tray, #318, round, Florentine Green, 6½"w, 4"h, $75.00

PLATE 203. Butter Ball Tray, #318, oval, Velva Rose (pink), 5¾"–7"w, 4½"h, $85.00

PLATE 204. Server, handled, oval, Tangerine, 8¼"–10½"w, 5"h, 5¾"b, scarce shape, $125.00 ($60.00 blue)

PLATE 205. Server, #317, handled, round, cupped rim, Celeste Blue, 9½"w, 5"h, 3½"b, scarce shape, $70.00

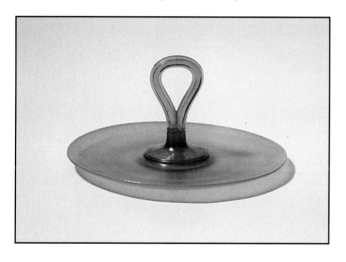

PLATE 206. Server, #317, handled, round, Tangerine, 10½"w, 5¼"h, 3½"b, scarce color, $125.00 ($60.00 blue)

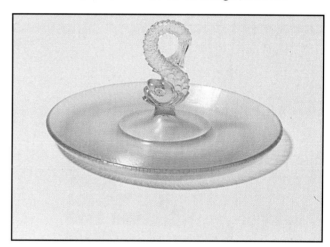

PLATE 207. Butter Ball Tray, #1557, round, dolphin-handled, Florentine Green, 6½"w, 3½"h, scarce shape, $140.00

PLATE 208. Server, round, dolphin-handled, Velva Rose (pink), 10¼"w, 4½"h, 3¼"b, scarce shape, $125.00

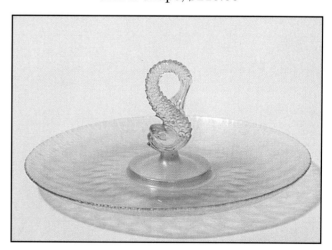

PLATE 209. Server, #1502A, round, dolphin-handled, diamond optic, Florentine Green, 10½"w, 4½"h, 3¼"b, scarce shape, $150.00

PLATE 210. Cheese & Cracker Set, #316, Topaz with gold etched decoration; Cheese Dish, 4⅞"w, 2½"h, 3¼"b; Plate, 10"w, 4½"b, $65.00 set

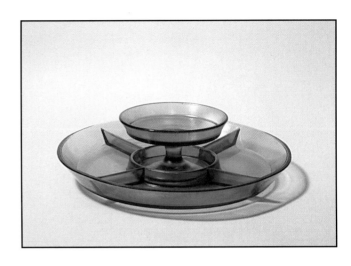

PLATE 211. Sweet Meat Set, #1647, Celeste Blue, rare shape; Cheese Dish, 4¾"w, 2½"h, 3⅜"b; Plate 10¼"w, 1⅜"h, 3½"b, $90.00 set

PLATE 212. Candy Jar, #8, ½-lb, Wisteria (light purple), 3⅝"w, 7¾"h, 3"b, $60.00 ($40.00 blue)

PLATE 213. Candy Jar, #9, ¾-lb, Ruby (red), 4"w, 9"h, 3½"b, rare color, $240.00 ($50.00 blue)

PLATE 214. Candy Jar, #9, ¾-lb, Persian Pearl (crystal) with black decoration, 4"w, 9"h, 3½"b, rare decoration, $150.00

PLATE 215. Candy Jar, #9, ¾-lb, Topaz with paint decoration, 4"w, 9"h, 3½"b, scarce decoration, $55.00

PLATE 216. Candy Jar, #9, ¾-lb, Celeste Blue
with grape wheel cut and gold trim,
4"w, 9"h, 3½"b, scarce decoration, $60.00

PLATE 217. Candy Jar, #1533A, ¾-lb, twin-
dolphin, Aquamarine, 4"w, 9"h, 3½"b, $125.00,
rare color; Candy Jar, #1532A, ½-lb, twin-
dolphin, Tangerine, 3⅝"w, 7¾"h, 3"b,
scarce color, $150.00

PLATE 218. Candy Jar, #835, ½-lb,
Tangerine, 4¼"w, 9½"h, 3"b, $80.00

PLATE 219. Candy Jar, #635, ½-lb, Velva Rose
(pink), 3¾"w, 8¼"h, 3¼"b, scarce shape, $60.00

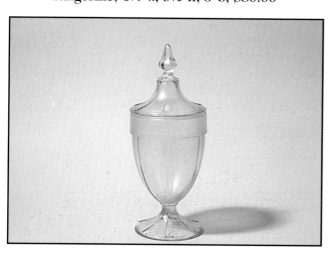

PLATE 220. Candy Jar, #636, 1-lb,
Persian Pearl (crystal), 4¼"w, 10"h, 3⅞"b, $50.00

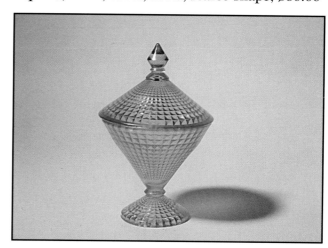

PLATE 221. Candy Jar, #568, ½-lb,
diamond optic, Florentine Green,
5"w, 7½"h, 3⅛"b, $45.00

57

PLATE 222. Candy Jar, #735, ½-lb, rib optic, Wisteria (light purple), 5"w, 7½"h, 3⅛"b, $60.00

PLATE 223. Candy Jar, #736, 1-lb, rib optic, Topaz, 6"w, 8¾"h, 3¾"b, $60.00

PLATE 224. Candy Jar, #736, 1-lb, rib optic, Ruby (red), 6"w, 8¾"h, 3¾"b, rare color, $800.00

PLATE 225. Bonbon, #543, Velva Rose (dark pink/brown), 5⅜"w, 4¾"h, 2¾"b, $50.00

PLATE 226. Bonbon, Velva Rose (pink), 5⅜"w, 4¾"h, 2¾"b, $60.00

PLATE 227. Bonbon, #844, 1-lb, flower top, Aquamarine, 6¼"w, 6½"h, 3¼"b, rare undamaged, $180.00

PLATE 228. Bonbon, #643, 1-lb, Wisteria (light purple), 5¼"w, 6¼"h, 3½"b, scarce color, $70.00

PLATE 229. Bonbon, #943, ½-lb, round stem, Velva Rose (pink), 5¼"w, 6"h, 3½"b, $55.00

PLATE 230. Bonbon, #1043, 1-lb, octagon stem, Celeste Blue, 6¼"w, 6"h, 3¼"b, $70.00

PLATE 231. Bonbon, #10, Tangerine, 4¼"w, 6½"h, 4⅜"b, scarce shape/color, $150.00

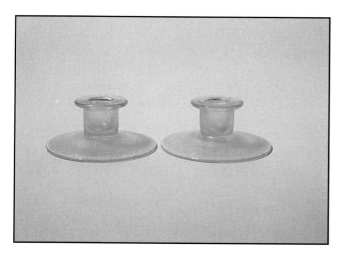

PLATE 232. Candlesticks, #314, Topaz, 1⅝"h, 4"b, $30.00 pair

PLATE 233. Candlesticks, #318, Topaz, 2¾"h, 4⅜"b, $50.00 pair

PLATE 234. Candlesticks, #317,
Florentine Green, 3¾"h, 5"b, $60.00 pair

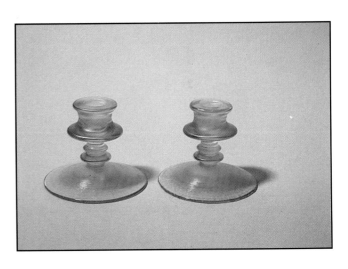

PLATE 235. Candlesticks, #316, two rings on
stem (early), Persian Pearl (crystal), 3½"h, 4¼"b,
rare shape, $90.00 pair

PLATE 236. Candlesticks, #316, one ring on
stem (late), Tangerine, 3⅜"h, 4¼"b, $60.00 pair

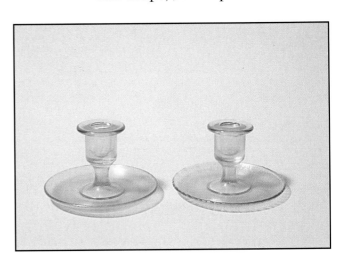

PLATE 237. Candlesticks, #315,
Florentine Green, 3¼"h, 5"b, $60.00 pair

PLATE 238. Candlesticks, #315 variation,
Wisteria (light purple), 3⅛"h, 5⅛"b, $150.00 pair

PLATE 239. Candlesticks, #1623,
twin-dolphin, Wisteria (light purple),
3½"h, 3⅞"b, $225.00 pair

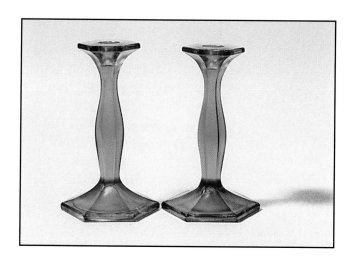

PLATE 240. Candlesticks, #249,
Celeste Blue, 6½"h, 3½"b, $60.00 pair

PLATE 241. Candlesticks, #249,
Royal Blue (cobalt blue), 6½"h, 3½"b,
rare color, $200.00 pair

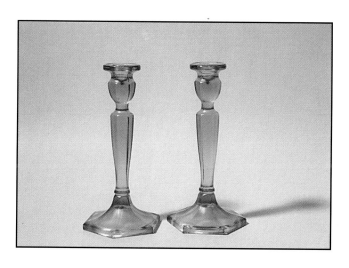

PLATE 242. Candlesticks, #449,
Velva Rose (pink), 8⅝"h, 3⅞"b, scarce color,
$125.00 pair ($80.00 blue)

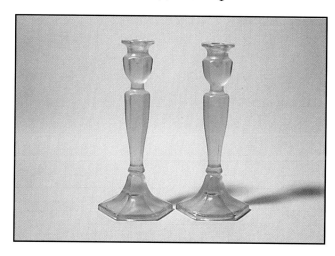

PLATE 243. Candlesticks, #349, Topaz,
10½"h, 4⅛"b, $120.00 pair

PLATE 244. Candlesticks, #349, Ruby (red),
10½"h, 4⅛"b, rare color, $650.00 pair

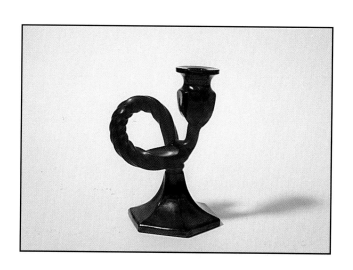

PLATE 245. Candlesticks, #349, whimsey,
Ruby (red), 7½"h, 4⅛"b, only one known, $250.00

PLATE 246. Candlesticks, #232,
Wisteria (light purple), 8½"h, 4"b,
$200.00 pair ($125.00 blue)

PLATE 247. Candlesticks, #549,
Celeste Blue, 8⅛"h, 3¾"b, $140.00 pair

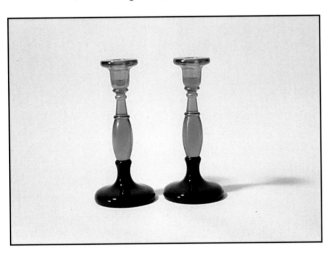

PLATE 248. Candlesticks, #549, black foot,
Celeste Blue, 8¼"h, 3¾"b, rare with black foot,
$250.00 pair

PLATE 249. Candlesticks, #649,
Wisteria (light purple), 9"h, 4"b,
$200.00 pair ($150.00 blue)

PLATE 250. Candlesticks, #950,
Aquamarine, 6"h, 2½" x 4"b, $180.00 pair

PLATE 251. Candle Vase, #1673,
Florentine Green, 7¼"h, 4½"b,
only one known, $350.00

PLATE 252. Cream and Sugar Set, rib optic,
Topaz, 3⅜"w, 2¼"h, 1¾"b, $125.00 set

PLATE 253. Cream and Sugar Set, #2,
Florentine Green with cobalt handles; Creamer,
2⅝"w, 3½"h, 3⅛"b; Sugar, 3⅝"w, 3"h, 3½"b,
$200.00 set

PLATE 254. Cream and Sugar Set, #3,
Tangerine, 3⅝"w, 3½"h, 2½"b, $120.00 set

PLATE 255. Cream and Sugar Set, #1502,
diamond optic, Celeste Blue, 3⅝"w, 3½"h, 2½"b,
$135.00 set

PLATE 256. Bridge Goblet, #1502,
diamond optic, Velva Rose (pink),
3⅛"w, 6⅛"h, 3"b, scarce shape, $110.00 each

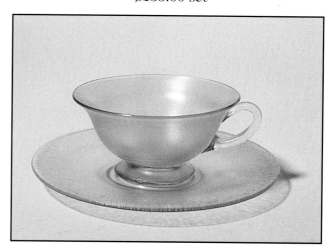

PLATE 257. Cup and Saucer Set, Velva
Rose (pink); Cup, 4½"w, 2⅛"h, 2⅛"b;
Saucer/Plate, round, 6¾"w, 2½"b, $100.00 set

PLATE 258. Night Set, #401, Tumble Up, Wisteria (light purple), scarce color; Jug, 3¾"w, 5¾"h, 2½"b; Glass, 2¼"w, 2⅞"h, 2"b, $150.00 set ($75.00 blue)

PLATE 259. Night Set, #1502, Celeste Blue; Jug, 3¾"w, 5⅞"h, 3⅛"b; Glass for #401 Night Set, $100.00

PLATE 260. Guest Set, #200, Florentine Green with cobalt handle; Jug, 3"w, 7"h, 2¾"b; Tumbler, 2¼"w, 3⅜"h, 3"b, $400.00 set ($300.00 pink)

PLATE 261. Guest Set, #200, Tangerine with tangerine handle; Jug, 3"w, 7"h, 2¾"b; Tumbler, 2¼"w, 3⅝"h, 3"b, $600.00 set

PLATE 262. Guest Set, #200, curtain optic, Topaz with cobalt handle; Jug, 3"w, 7"h, 2¾"b; Tumbler, 2¼"w, 3⅝"h, 3"b, $650.00 set

PLATE 263. Pitcher and Tumblers Set, Celeste Blue with blue handle; Pitcher, 4¾"w, 6⅞"h, 3⅝"b; Tumblers, 2½"w, 3¾"h, 2"b, $350.00 set

PLATE 264. Pitcher and Tumbler Set, #220, rib optic, 8 piece, Celeste Blue with crystal handles, scarce handle color; Pitcher with Cover, 5"w, 9¾"h, 4⅛"b; Tumbler, #222, 10-oz. Ice Tea, 3¼"w, 4⅜"h, 2"b, $650.00 set

PLATE 265. Pitcher and Tumbler Set, #220, rib optic, Wisteria (light purple) with cobalt handles, $750.00 set; Pitcher with Cover, 5"w, 9¾"h, 4⅛"b; Tumbler, #220, 12-oz Lemon Aid, with wheel cut design, 3"w, 5⅛"h, 2¼"b; Pitcher Base, cobalt blue, $50.00 each; Coaster, cobalt blue, $15.00 each

PLATE 266. Pitcher and Tumbler Set, #215 Juice, Florentine Green; Pitcher, 2 ¾"w, 8¼"h, 3½"b, $200.00; Tumbler, 2⅛"w, 3⅝"h, 1⅝"b, $50.00 each

PLATE 267. Pitcher and Tumbler, Florentine Green; Pitcher, 4"w, 9¼"h, 5⅝"b, $150.00; Tumbler, 3"w, 5¼"h, 2¼"b, $50.00

PLATE 268. Pitcher and Tumbler Set, #222, rib optic, Celeste Blue with cobalt blue handles; Pitcher (does not come with cover), 4¾"w, 10"h, 3⅝"b; Tumbler, 3"w, 5¼"h, 2¼"b, $500.00 set

PLATE 269. Pitcher and Tumbler, #222, curtain optic, Topaz with topaz handle; Pitcher, 4⅞"w, 10⅛"h, 3⅝"b, $600.00; Tumbler, 3"w, 5⅛"h, 2¼"b, $150.00

PLATE 270. Pitcher and Tumbler, #222, curtain optic, Topaz with cobalt blue handle; Pitcher, 4⅞"w, 10⅛"h, 3⅝"b, $1,000.00; Tumbler, 3"w, 5⅛"h, 2¼"b, $150.00

PLATE 271. Pitcher and Tumbler, 4-ringed base, Grecian Gold (marigold) with cobalt blue handle, wheel cut design; Pitcher, 3½"w, 8¼"h, 3¾"b, $350.00; Tumbler, 2⅜"w, 3⅝"h, 1¾"b, $100.00

PLATE 272. Pitcher, 4-ringed base, Persian Pearl (crystal) with cobalt blue handle, 3½"w, 8¼"h, 3¾"b, $400.00

PLATE 273. Pitcher and Tumbler, 4-ringed base, curtain optic, Topaz with topaz handle; Pitcher, 3½"w, 8¼"h, 3¾"b, $450.00; Tumbler, 2⅜"w, 3⅝"h, 1¾"b, $250.00

PLATE 274. Pitcher and Tumbler, 4-ring base, rib optic, Topaz with cobalt blue handle; Pitcher, 3½"w, 8¼"h, 3¾"b, $450.00; Tumbler, 2⅝"w, 5⅜"h, 2"b, $150.00

PLATE 275. Pitchers, 4-ringed base, curtain optic, Topaz with cobalt blue handles; Small, 3½"w, 8¼"h, 3¾"b, $450.00; Medium, 3¾"w, 9¼"h, 4⅛"b, $450.00; Large, 3⅞"w, 10¼"h, 4⅝"b, $450.00

PLATE 276. Nut Cup Set, #923, Celeste blue;
Master Cup, 5⅜"w, 4"h, 3⅝"b; Individual Cups,
2¼"w, 2⅛"h, 1½"b, $450.00 set

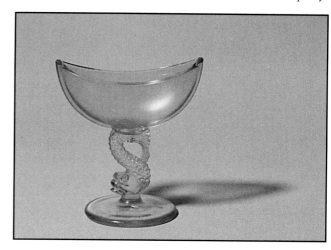

PLATE 277. Nut Cup, oval, dolphin-stem,
Florentine Green, 2⅛" x 4⅜"w, 4⅝"h, 2¾"b,
rare shape, $600.00

PLATE 278. Ice Cream, footed,
Celeste Blue, 4¾"w, 2½"h, 2⅜"b,
rare shape, $100.00

PLATE 279. Salt, #923, Persian Pearl (crystal),
3⅜"w, 1½"h, 1½"b, $50.00

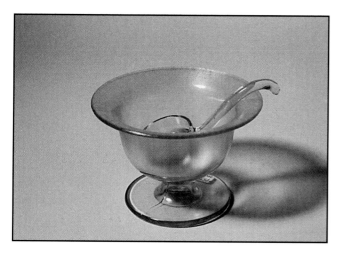

PLATE 280. Mayonnaise, #923, ladle (should be
iridized), Aquamarine, 5½"w, 3¾"h, 3¾"b,
rare color, $100.00 set ($65.00 blue)

PLATE 281. Toothpick or Pen Holder,
Florentine Green, 2"w, 2⅝"h, 1½"b,
desirable shape, $300.00

PLATE 282. Lemon Tray, handled, #66,
Velva Rose (pink), 4⅞"w, 2¼"h, rare color,
$100.00

PLATE 283. Lemon Tray, handled, #66,
Topaz with paint decoration, 4⅞"w, 2¼"h, $45.00

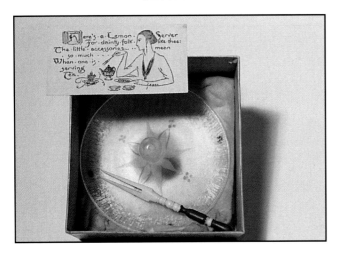

PLATE 284. Lemon Tray, handled #66,
in original box with fork, Topaz with paint
decoration, $80.00 set

PLATE 285. Ash Tray 5-Piece Set, #202,
4 inserts, Celeste Blue, 5"w, 1⅛"h, $160.00 set

PLATE 286. Cigarette Holder, #554, round,
Velva Rose (pink), 2"w, 3¼"h, 4¾"b, $150.00

PLATE 287. Cigarette Holder, #556, oval,
Florentine Green, 2½"w, 3¼"h, 4¾"b, $150.00

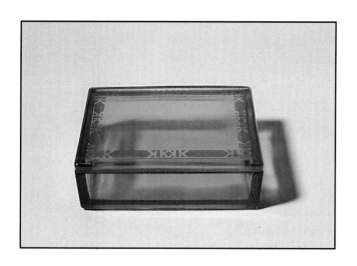

PLATE 288. Cigarette Box, #655, Celeste Blue
with wheel cutting, 3⅜" x 4⅜"w, 1½"h,
scarce shape, $150.00

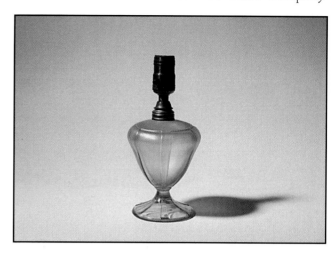

PLATE 289. Lamp, Velva Rose (pink),
4⅜"w, 5¾"h, 3⅞"b, only one known, $200.00

PLATE 290. Basket, #1620, handled,
Plymouth Line, Persian Pearl (crystal),
10⅝"w, 5⅛"h, 3¾"b, $200.00

PLATE 291. Basket, #1616, diamond optic,
Velva Rose (pink), 9"w, 6"h, 3½"b, $150.00

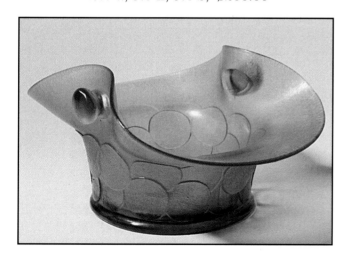

PLATE 292. Basket, #1681, Big Cookie,
Amber, 10¾"w, 5⅛"h, 5⅝"b, only one known,
$400.00

PLATE 293. Cologne, #53, diamond optic,
Velva Rose (dark pink/brown), 1½"w, 5"h, 1¾"b,
$125.00

PLATE 294. Cologne and Puff Box, #53, diamond optic, Celeste Blue; Cologne, 1½"w, 5"h, 1¾"b, $125.00; Puff Box, 4¼"w, 3¾"h, 2½"b, $75.00

PLATE 295. Cologne, #54, Topaz, 1½"w, 5"h, 1¾"b, $110.00

PLATE 296. Puff Box, #54, Celeste Blue, 4¼"w, 3¾"h, 2½"b, $55.00

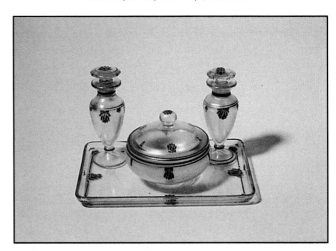

PLATE 297. Vanity Set, #54, Persian Pearl (crystal) with decoration, rare shape, $460.00 set; Cologne, 1½"w, 5"h, 1¾"b, $130.00; Puff Box, 4¼"w, 3¾"h, 2½"b, $80.00; Tray, 5⅞"x8½"w, ⅝"h, $120.00

PLATE 298. Cologne, #55, round finial stopper, Florentine Green, 1⅜"w, 6⅜"h, 1¾"b, $130.00

PLATE 299. Cologne, #55, pagoda finial stopper, Wisteria (light purple), 1⅜"w, 7"h, 1¾"b, scarce color, $175.00

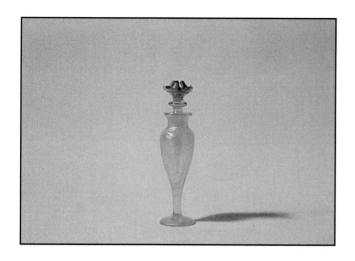

PLATE 300. Cologne, #55½, flower finial stopper, Topaz, 1⅜"w, 7"h, 1¾"b, scarce stopper, $250.00

PLATE 301. Cologne, #59, nipple finial stopper, Velva Rose (pink), 1⅜"w, 3⅝"h, 2¾"b, $170.00

PLATE 302. Cologne, #56, pagoda finial stopper, Florentine Green, 1⅜"w, 5⅜"h, 2⅜"b, $150.00

PLATE 303. Cologne, #56, nipple finial stopper, Celeste Blue, 1⅜"w, 5½"h, 2½"b, $140.00

PLATE 304. Bath Salts Jar, #60, pagoda top stopper, Wisteria (light purple), 3⅛"w, 4"h, 2⅝"b, $160.00

PLATE 305. Puff Box, mini size, nipple finial, Topaz, 3"w, 3¼"h, 1¾"b, rare shape, $80.00

71

PLATE 306. Puff Box, #57, nipple finial,
Florentine Green, 3½"w, 4⅛"h, 2⅛"b, $80.00

PLATE 307. Puff Box, #743, button finial,
Florentine Green, 5"w, 5¼"h, 2⅜"b, $60.00

PLATE 308. Puff Box, #744, flower finial,
Florentine Green, 5"w, 5¼"h, 2⅜"b, rare finial,
$100.00

PLATE 309. Puff Box, Velva Rose (pink),
6"w, 3¾"h, 3⅞"b, scarce shape, $125.00

PLATE 310. Puff Box, Florentine Green,
4½"w, 3⅞"h, 3¾"b, rare shape, $90.00

PLATE 311. Bath Jar, #16, narrow mouth,
Velva Rose (pink), 1⅜"w, 4½"h, 2½" sq. b,
$100.00

PLATE 312. Bath Jar, #17, wide mouth,
Florentine Green, 2¼"w, 4½"h, 2½" sq. b,
$100.00

PLATE 313. Shaving Mug, #630,
Celeste Blue, 3⅝"w, 3½"h, 3⅛"b, rare shape,
only blue and topaz known, $600.00

PLATE 314. Flower Pot and Under-Plate, #1554,
Tangerine, scarce shape; Flower Pot, 4¾"w, 4⅝"h,
3⅛"b, $100.00; Plate, 6⅛"w, 1⅜"h, 4¼"b, $75.00

PLATE 315. Vase, Fan (miniature), from #53
Cologne, diamond optic, Celeste Blue,
1" x 3⅜"w, 4¼"h, 1¾"b, only one known, $200.00

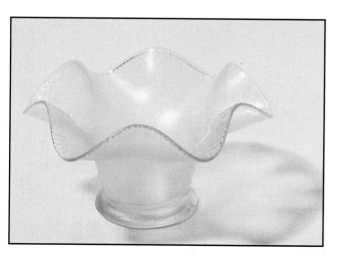

PLATE 316. Vase, #106, crimped,
Persian Pearl (crystal), 6"w, 3¼"h, 2⅝"b, $40.00

PLATE 317. Vase, #612, flared, Tangerine,
6"w, 6¼"h, 3½"b, $80.00

PLATE 318. Vase, #1502 (6"), diamond optic, cupped, Celeste Blue, 3½"w, 5¼"h, 2¾"b, $60.00

PLATE 319. Vase, #1502 (8"), diamond optic, flared, Tangerine, 7¼"w, 8¼"h, 4"b, $150.00

PLATE 320. Vase, #621, flared, Ruby (red), 7⅞"w, 8"h, 4"b, rare color, $300.00

PLATE 321. Vase, #621, flared, crimped, Celeste Blue, 8⅜"w, 8¼"h, 4"b, $175.00

PLATE 322. Vase, #621, cupped, Ruby (red), 5¾"w, 8⅜"h, 4"b, $200.00

PLATE 323. Vase, #621, hat shaped, Topaz, 12¼"w, 4¾"h, 4"b, $110.00

PLATE 324. Vase, Florentine Green with decoration 3"w, 7½"h, 2½"b, scarce decoration, $150.00

PLATE 325. Vase, #1700, Sheffield, oval, Aquamarine, 7¾"w, 8⅛"h, 3¼"b, $160.00

PLATE 326. Vase, flared, cupped, curtain optic, Topaz, 6¼"w, 7"h, 4⅛"b, $300.00

PLATE 327. Vase, flared, curtain optic, Topaz, 7¼"w, 9¼"h, 3½"b, $700.00

PLATE 328. Vase, flared, 4-ringed base, rib optic, Topaz with cobalt blue crest, 4⅝"w, 8"h, 4"b, $600.00

PLATE 329. Vase, flared, 4-ringed base, rib optic, Topaz with cobalt blue crest and handles, 5"w, 9"h, 4"b, only two known, $750.00

PLATE 330. Vase, #891, ribbed, Royal Blue
(cobalt blue), 3½"w, 12"h, 2⅞"b, $750.00

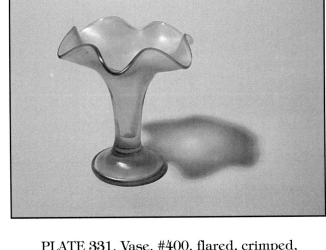

PLATE 331. Vase, #400, flared, crimped,
Florentine Green, 5¼"w, 5½"h, 3"b, $40.00

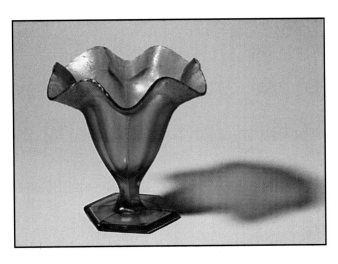

PLATE 332. Vase, #574, flared, crimped,
Celeste Blue, 5⅞"w, 5⅝"h, 3"b, $65.00

PLATE 333. Vase, #835, 6-sided, Tangerine,
5⅛"w, 5½"h, 3"b, rare color, $75.00

PLATE 334. Vase, #572, fan, rib optic,
Florentine Green, 6¼"w, 8½"h, 3¾"b, $40.00

PLATE 335. Vase, #573, 6-sided, rib optic,
Velva Rose (pink), 5⅛"w, 8"h, 3¾"b, $45.00

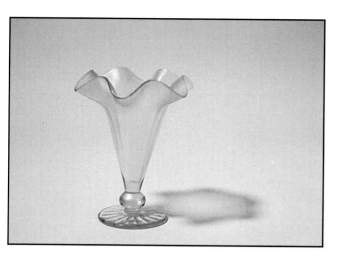

PLATE 336. Vase, #573, flared crimped, rib optic, Aquamarine, 6½"w, 8"h, 3¾"b, scarce color, $85.00

PLATE 337. Vase, #562, flared, rib optic, Celeste Blue, 5¼"w, 8"h, 3⅝"b, scarce shape, $75.00

PLATE 338. Vase, flared, rolled rim, Celeste Blue with decoration, 5½"w, 6⅜"h, 3½"b rare shape, $75.00

PLATE 339. Vase, Cornucopia, flared, Topaz, 5½"w, 7½"h, 3½"b, rare shape, $100.00

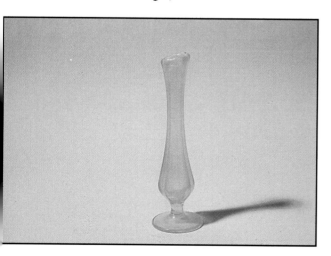

PLATE 340. Vase, #354, short bud, Topaz, 1¼"w, 7¼"h, 2⅛"b, $35.00

PLATE 341. Vase, #99, flared bud, Celeste Blue, 1⅝"w, 7¼"h, 3"b, $35.00

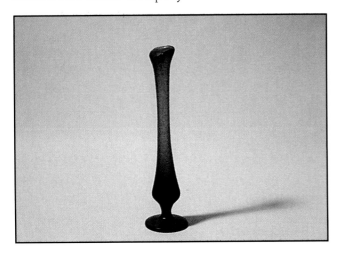

PLATE 342. Vase, #251, bud, Wisteria
(light purple), 1⅝"w, 11¼"h, 2¾"b, scarce color,
$80.00

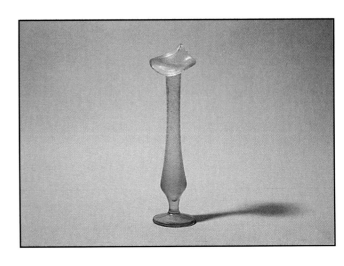

PLATE 343. Vase, #251, bud, "Jack-in-the-Pulpit," Florentine Green, 3"w, 11¼"h, 2¾"b,
scarce shape, $60.00

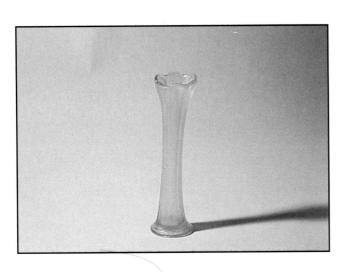

PLATE 344. Vase, Florentine Green,
3¼"w, 11½"h, 3¼"b, $100.00

PLATE 345. Vase, #1530, ring optic,
Tangerine, 4⅝"w, 11¼"h, 3⅛"b, $125.00

PLATE 346. Vase, #1531, ring optic,
Celeste Blue, 6"w, 15"h, 3⅝"b, $175.00

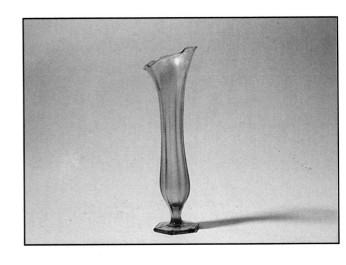

PLATE 347. Vase, #574, swung, flared,
Velva Rose (pink), 4"w, 12½"h, 3"b, $75.00

PLATE 348. Vase, #567, fan, diamond optic,
Velva Rose (pink), 6"w, 5¼"h, 3⅛"b, $50.00

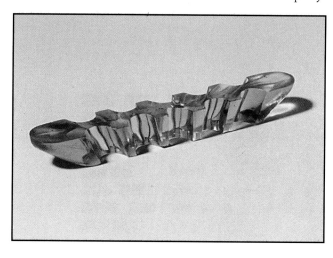

PLATE 349. Frog, for fan vase (not iridized),
¾"w, 5½" long, ⅝"b, $50.00

PLATE 350. Vase, #1532A, twin-dolphin,
Aquamarine, 5½"w, 5⅛"h, 3"b, rare color,
$100.00

PLATE 351. Vase, #1533A, twin-dolphin,
Tangerine, 6⅜"w, 6"h, 3½"b, rare color,
$100.00

PLATE 352. Vase, #1502A, twin-dolphin,
diamond optic, Florentine Green,
6⅜"w, 6"h, 3½"b, $90.00

PLATE 353. Vase, #736, fan, rib optic,
Wisteria (light purple), 7¼"w, 6"h, 3¾"b,
$70.00

79

PLATE 354. Vase, #570, fan, rib optic,
Topaz with etching and gold decoration,
7"w, 5⅞"h, 3½"b, $50.00

PLATE 355. Vase, #847, Melon-Rib,
Tangerine, 6⅛"w, 4¾"h, 3¼"b, $75.00

PLATE 356. Vase, #847, fan, Melon-Rib,
Aquamarine, 8⅜"w, 5¾"h, 3¼"b, $60.00

PLATE 357. Vase, #857, fan, Melon-Rib,
very light purple, 10½"w, 7⅝"h, 4"b,
unique color, $150.00

IMPERIAL GLASS COMPANY

Bellaire, Ohio

Imperial Glass Co., Bellaire, Ohio, made several lines of glass which we would call stretch glass today. In their advertisements, they used the terms Satin Iridescent Line, NUART, and simply Imperial Art Glass. At no time in their advertisements did they refer to their stretch glass or art glass as Imperial Jewels. Imperial Jewels appears to be a term that caught on even during the time of stretch glass production. The name's origin appears to be the result of descriptions printed in various trade journals of the time.

In the Imperial advertisements, as published by Margaret and Douglas Archer (1978), numerous photographic examples of stretch glass are represented, often with Ice, crizzled satin, satin iridescent and bright iridescent being used as descriptives.

Imperial colors are probably some of the most difficult to identify because the color names used by Imperial often do not fit the current usage of the names.

Satin Iridescent Colors –
Amber Ice – crizzled on amber glass – a light brown glass (Plate 406).
Amethyst Ice – crizzled on mulberry glass – a light purple glass, a wisteria (Plate 360).
black – this may actually be their Purple Glaze which was described as "A very brilliant blue iridescent effect, on dark amethyst glass." Probably not stretched though satiny pieces have been seen (not illustrated).
Blue Ice – blue crizzled on crystal glass – the blue smoke stretch (Plate 388).
Green Ice – crizzled on green glass – actually a blue-green glass or teal stretch (Plate 359).
Iris Ice – white crizzled on crystal glass – white or pearl stretch (Plate 358).
ruby and amberina – red stretch known, but not named in this line (Plate 362).
Rose Ice – pink crizzled on crystal glass – most likely a light marigold stretch (Plate 365).
pink – pink glass with white or pearl iridescence (Plate 413).
pink marigold – pink glass with marigold iridescence (Plate 384).
pink smoke – pink glass with blue smoke iridescence (Plate 383).
Blue Glow – similar to Sapphire (see below), being crystal glass with a blue-gray iridescence, usually satin effect (not illustrated).
Red Glow – similar to Nuruby (see below), being crystal glass with a yellow-orange iridescence, usually satin effect (not illustrated).

Other Colors –
Associated with the Imperial Art Glass line (e.g., Imperial Jewels); pieces often have the Imperial Iron Cross impressed in the bottom or NUART.

Pearl Amethyst – a medium purple glass with multicolor iridescence (Plate 369)
Pearl Green – light green glass with green-gray iridescence (Plate 378).
Pearl Ruby – crystal glass with a heavy yellow-orange iridescence – a deep marigold (Plate 375).
Pearl Silver – a dark purple glass with silver iridescence (Plate 377).
Pearl White – crystal glass with white iridescence (Plate 370).
marigold milk – a milk glass with rich orange-red iridescence, not named in this line (Plate 380).
blue smoke milk – a milk glass with blue-gray iridescence, probably the same as used in Blue Ice, not named in this line (Plates 381 & 459).

Colors associated with Bright Iridescent Colors that are considered Imperial carnival glass colors though several advertising pages list these colors and show obvious stretch pieces.

Peacock Iridescent – crystal glass with a gold-yellow iridescence – a light yellowish marigold, clambroth of carnival glass (not illustrated).
Rubigold Iridescent – crystal glass with a deep yellow-orange iridescence – a deep marigold; proba-

bly not used on stretch glass because the iridescence was designed for heavily figured glass, i.e., carnival (not illustrated).

Nuruby Iridescent – crystal glass with a deep yellow-orange iridescence – a deep marigold; most likely the same as Pearl Ruby but used on more common Imperial glass pieces; unfortunately, many think that this is the Imperial ruby or red stretch and carnival (not illustrated).

Sapphire – crystal glass with a blue-gray iridescence – called smoke; most likely the same iridescence as Blue Ice (not illustrated).

Azur – dark, almost black-amethyst glass with multicolored iridescence; most likely used in carnival glass but a couple of pieces of 'black' stretch glass are known though the stretch effect is usually more satin in effect (not illustrated).

Purple Glaze – dark amethyst glass with a royal blue iridescence; most likely used in carnival glass but a couple of plain pieces are known with blue iridescence but no stretch or satin effect (not illustrated).

Helios – medium green glass with silvery, mirror-like iridescence; only seen in carnival (not illustrated).

The most common Imperial stretch colors seem to be their marigolds (e.g., Rose Ice, Pearl Ruby, and Nuruby) and crystals (e.g., Iris Ice and Pearl White). The blue smoke stretch (e.g., Blue Ice and Sapphire), amber, and wisteria are much less common, as is the red-amberina stretch (actual name unknown). Imperial's red stretch is some of the best around since the iridescence was generally applied to both inner and outer surfaces. The Green Ice is a unique blue-green glass (teal, in modern color terms) which is moderately available.

In the Imperial Art Glass lines, all the colors are fairly common except for the Pearl Green, marigold milk, and blue smoke milk. All of these are considered to be the true Imperial Jewels and most have outstanding iridescence and stretch effects, making them highly collectible.

+ = Imperial "Iron Cross" mark present

PLATE 358. Bowl, #22/93, flared, optic 3-paneled Wide Panel, Iris Ice (crystal), 6"w, 2⅜"h, 2⅝"b, $35.00

PLATE 359. Bowl, round, optic 12-paneled Wide Panel, Green Ice (blue-green), 8¼"w, 3¼"h, 3¼"b, $50.00

PLATE 360. Bowl, flared, optic 12-paneled
Wide Panel, Amethyst Ice (light purple),
9"w, 3¼"h, 3¼"b, $65.00

PLATE 361. Bowl, #22/73, wide flared,
optic 12-paneled Wide Panel, red,
9¾"w, 2¼"h, 3¼"b, $175.00

PLATE 362. Bowl, flared,
optic 14-paneled Smooth Panels, red,
9¾"w, 4"h, 4½"b, $180.00

PLATE 363. Bowl, wide flared,
10-paneled Smooth Panels, Iris Ice (crystal),
12¾"w, 4½"h, 5¼"b, $80.00

PLATE 364. Bowl, flared, optic 16-paneled
Wide Panel, Green Ice (blue-green),
10½"w, 3¼"h, 5⅝"b, $70.00

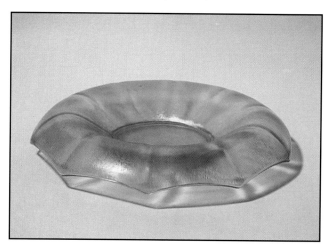

PLATE 365. Bowl, #7287, rolled rim,
10-paneled, Rays and Points, Rose Ice (light
marigold), 13¼"w, 2⅛"h, 5⅞"b, $65.00

PLATE 366. Bowl, #7257, 2-handled, shallow,
10-paneled, pink smoke with decoration,
11¾"w, 3h", 6¾"b, $125.00

PLATE 367. Bowl, #7287, footed, flared,
8-paneled, Rays and Points, Rose Ice (light
marigold), 10¾"w, 3¼"h, 4½"b, $85.00

PLATE 368. Bowl, #719, wide cupped,
ribbed, Iris Ice (crystal), 9⅜"w, 2"h, 3¾"b,
rare shape, $50.00

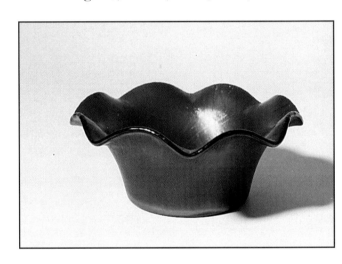

PLATE 369. Bowl, #63 Art Glass, bonbon,
crimped, Pearl Amethyst (purple), +,
5½"w, 2¼"h, 2¾"b, $100.00

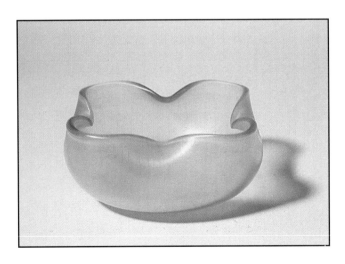

PLATE 370. Bowl, #38 Art Glass, bonbon,
square, Pearl White (crystal), +,
5½"w, 2¼"h, 2¾"b, $70.00

PLATE 371. Bowl, #65 Art Glass,
wide flared, Pearl Amethyst (purple), +,
5⅞"w, 1⅝"h, 3"b, $125.00

84

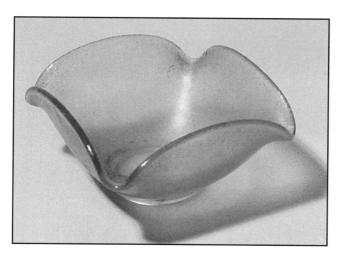

PLATE 372. Bowl, #34 Art Glass, berry,
square, Pearl White (crystal), +,
6¾"w, 2¾"h, 2½"b, $60.00

PLATE 373. Bowl, Art Glass, cupped,
Pearl Ruby (marigold) with decoration, +,
5"w, 2¼"h, 2⅜"b, $125.00

PLATE 374. Bowl, #88 Art Glass, cupped,
Pearl Green (light green), +, 6⅜"w, 2"h, 5⅜"b,
$100.00

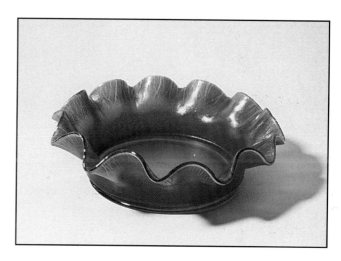

PLATE 375. Bowl, Art Glass, crimped,
Pearl Ruby (marigold), +, 8"w, 2¼"h, 5¼"b,
$125.00

PLATE 376. Bowl, #42 Art Glass, flower,
Pearl Ruby (marigold), +, 7¾"w, 2⅜"h, 3⅛"b,
$90.00

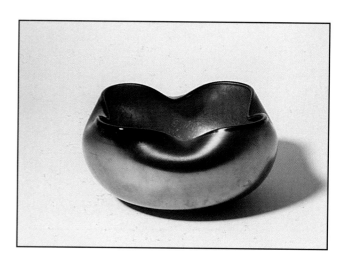

PLATE 377. Bowl, #70 Art Glass, square,
crimped, Pearl Silver (dark purple),
8"w, 3¾"h, 4"b, $140.00

PLATE 378. Bowl, #76 Art Glass, flower, flared, Pearl Green (light green), +, 9¾"w, 3¾"h, 3¾"b, $150.00

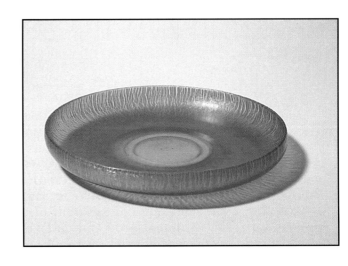

PLATE 379. Bowl, #57 Art Glass, wide cupped, Pearl Ruby (marigold), +, 11"w, 1⅝"h, 4"b, $150.00

PLATE 380. Bowl, cupped, marigold milk, 8⅜"w, 3⅝"h, 4"b, rare color, $175.00

PLATE 381. Bowl, wide flared, blue smoke milk, 10¾"w, 2¾"h, 4"b, rare color, $150.00

PLATE 382. Bowl, flared, marigold milk with decal decoration, 9¼"w, 4⅜"h, 3½"b, rare color, $175.00

PLATE 383. Bowl, #615, 2-handled Olive, oval, pink smoke, 2⅝"w, 1¾"h, 2½"b, scarce shape/color, $125.00

PLATE 384. Bowl, #84B, flared,
3-footed, pink marigold, 7½"w, 2½"h,
scarce shape, $60.00

PLATE 385. Bowl, #5141, flared,
3-footed, Floral and Optic, Green Ice
(blue-green), 8⅞"w, 3½"h, 2⅛"b, $125.00

PLATE 386. Bowl, #320, low footed, Double
Scroll, red, 9"x10¾"w, 4½"h, 3½" x 4½"b, $225.00
($90.00 Blue Ice, $150.00 Green Ice)

PLATE 387. Comport and Plate Set, red;
Comport, #600, flared, 18 rays,
6⅛"w, 4½"h, 3¾"b, $125.00; Plate, #645,
14-paneled, 8⅛"w, 4"b, $100.00

PLATE 388. Comport, cupped, crimped,
18 rays, Blue Ice (blue smoke),
4⅝"w, 4¾"h, 3¾"b, $50.00

PLATE 389. Comport, flared, rolled rim,
18 rays, red, 6½"w, 3½"h, 3¾"b, $130.00

PLATE 390. Comport, #582, footed jelly,
Iris Ice (crystal), 5"w, 5½"h, 3¼"b, $85.00

PLATE 391. Comport, flared, paneled,
Iris Ice (crystal), 4¾"w, 4⅞"h, 3¼"b, $85.00

PLATE 392. Comport, #44/50, flared,
18 rays, red, 7⅝"w, 7½"h, 4¾"b, $250.00

PLATE 393. Comport, #44/48, flared, cupped,
18 rays, Blue Ice (blue smoke), 8"w, 7"h, 4¾"b,
$125.00

PLATE 394. Comport, wide flared, crimped,
Iris Ice (crystal), 8¼"w, 7"h, 4¾"b, $90.00

PLATE 395. Comport, flattened tray,
Iris Ice (crystal), 9½"w, 5⅝"h, 4¾"b, $100.00

PLATE 396. Comport, flared, paneled,
Blue Ice (blue smoke),
10⅞"w, 7¼"h, 6¼"b, $110.00

PLATE 397. Comport, olive green,
8"w, 6½"h, 4"b, only one known, $175.00

PLATE 398. Comport, #727, or cheese dish,
pink marigold, 4¾"w, 3⅛"h, 3⅛"b, $55.00

PLATE 399. Sherbet and Under-Plate Set,
#600 Chesterfield, Rose Ice (marigold); Sherbet
4¼"w, 3¼"h, 2⅞"b, $30.00; Plate 6¼"w, 3"b, $15.00

PLATE 400. Sherbet, #499, optic rays,
red, 4"w, 3½"h, 2¾"b, $75.00

PLATE 401. Sherbet, #599, optic panels,
Green Ice (blue-green), 4¾"w, 3¾"h, 3"b, $50.00

PLATE 402. Sherbet, #499B,
Iris Ice (crystal), 4¾"w, 3⅝"h, 3"b, $25.00

PLATE 403. Plate, #499, optic rays,
red, 6⅛"w, 3⅜"b, $70.00

PLATE 404. Plate, Art Glass,
Pearl Amethyst (purple), +, 6½"w, 3"b, $110.00

PLATE 405. Plate, panels, star base,
light green, 8¼"w, 4"b, scarce color, $50.00

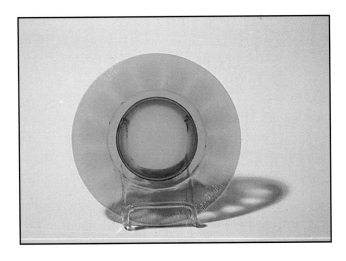

PLATE 406. Plate, #645, salad, optic 14-paneled,
Amber Ice (amber), 8⅛"w, 4"b, $40.00

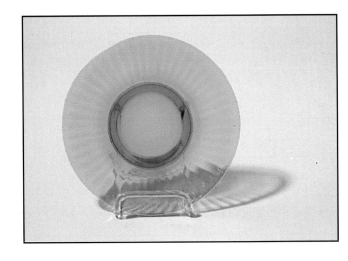

PLATE 407. Plate, #805, salad, 48 optic rays,
Green Ice (blue-green), 8¼"w, 4"b, $40.00

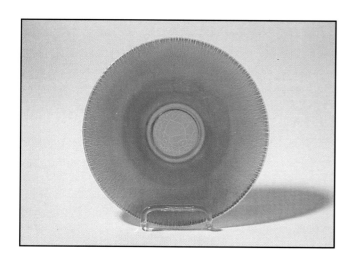

PLATE 408. Plate, #41 Art Glass,
Pearl Ruby (marigold), +, 9¾"w, 3"b, $100.00

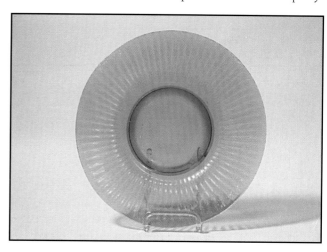

PLATE 409. Plate, #808, salad, 75 optic rays,
Green Ice (blue-green), 12"w, 5¾"b, $75.00

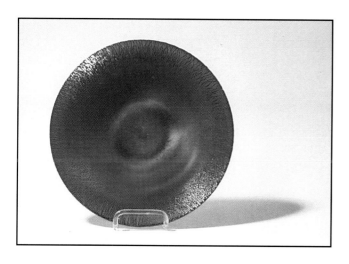

PLATE 410. Plate, #58 Art Glass,
sandwich, Pearl Amethyst (purple),
12½"w, 4"b, $150.00

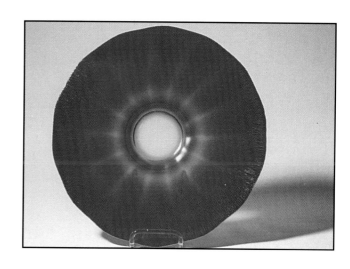

PLATE 411. Plate, #656, optic 14-paneled,
red, 14⅜"w, 4⅜"b, $300.00

PLATE 412. Plate, #7257, handled cake,
Iris Ice (crystal) with decal flowers,
10¼"w, 5⅝"b, $65.00

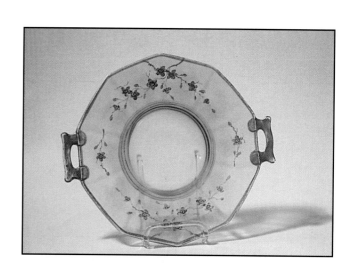

PLATE 413. Plate, #7257, handled cake,
pink with gold flowers and trim,
10¼"w, 5¾"b, $75.00

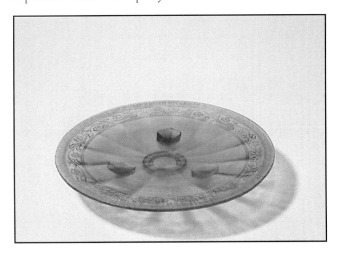

PLATE 414. Plate, 3-footed cake,
Floral and Optic, Green Ice (blue-green),
10¾"w, 2⅛"b, $125.00

PLATE 415. Tray, #7286, bread,
pink marigold, 12¼"w, 5"h, 4⅜"b, $80.00

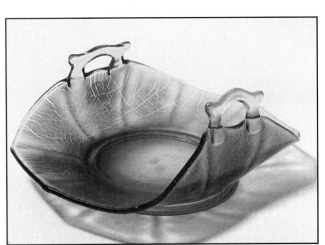

PLATE 416. Tray, #7257, bread, two-handled,
pink marigold, 10½"w, 4¼"h, 5⅝"b, $85.00

PLATE 417. Server, #664, handled,
Blue Ice (blue smoke), 10½"w, 4¼"h, 3¼"b, $50.00

PLATE 418. Server, #664, handled, #12 cut,
Blue Ice (blue smoke), 10½"w, 4¼"h, 3¼"b,
$75.00

PLATE 419. Server, #725, heart-handled fruit,
pink marigold with decal decoration,
11"w, 5"h, 3½"b, $100.00

PLATE 420. Cheese and Cracker Set, #461,
Blue Ice (blue smoke); Cheese Dish, 4½"w, 2⅞"h,
3⅜"b; Plate, 10¼"w, 5⅝"b, $75.00 set

PLATE 421. Mayonnaise and Under-Plate Set,
#313, optic swirl, Blue Ice (blue smoke); Bowl,
rolled rim, 6¾"w, 3¼"h, 3¼"b; Plate, 8"w, 4"b,
$90.00 set

PLATE 422. Mayonnaise and Under-Plate Set,
#4460, optic panels, Green Ice (blue-green);
Bowl, 10-paneled, 4⅝"w, 3"h, 2⅞"b; Plate,
14-paneled, 6½"w, 2⅞"b, $65.00 set

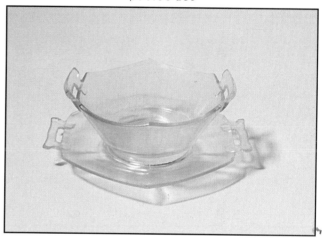

PLATE 423. Mayonnaise and Under-Plate Set,
#725, handled, Iris Ice (crystal); Bowl,
5⅞"w, 2½"h, 3¼"b; Plate, 7¼"w, 4"b, $90.00 set

PLATE 424. Covered Jar, #711, Iris Ice (crystal),
5⅝"w, 6⅝"h, 4½"b, rare shape, $125.00

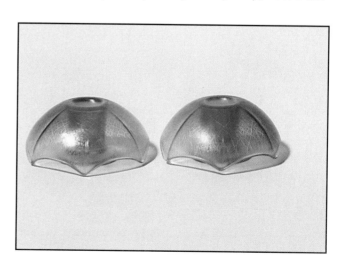

PLATE 425. Candlesticks, #727, rolled rim,
pink smoke, 4¼"w, 1⅞"h, 2¼"b, scarce color,
$150.00 pair

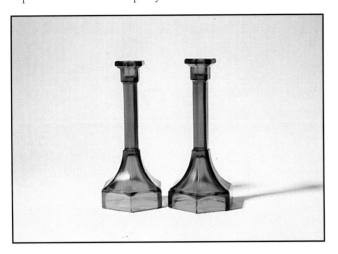

PLATE 426. Candlesticks, #6009,
Green Ice (blue-green), 9"h, 3¾"b, $150.00 pair

PLATE 427. Candlesticks, #320,
Double Scroll, Blue Ice (blue smoke),
8½"h, 3¾" x 4½"b, $115.00 pair

PLATE 428. Candlesticks, #635,
Premium with spiral optic bases,
Blue Ice (blue smoke), 8¾"h, 4⅛"b, $125.00 pair

PLATE 429. Candlestick/Bowl, Blue Ice
(blue smoke), 10⅛"w, 8"h, 3½"b, $125.00

PLATE 430. Cream and Sugar Set, #22/27,
rib optic, red; Creamer 3½"w, 3½"h, 2⅞"b;
Sugar 3¾"w, 3"h, 2⅞"b, $175.00 set

PLATE 431. Cream, Sugar, and Under-Plate Set,
pink smoke with decal decoration, rare shape;
Creamer, 3¼"w, 3"h, 2½"b; Sugar, 3¼"w, 2½"h,
2½"b; Plate, 9"w, 6"b, $250.00 set

PLATE 432. Cream and Sugar Set, Art Glass,
Pearl Amethyst (purple), scarce shape; Creamer,
4⅜"w, 2½"h, 2⅛"b; Sugar, 4⅜"w, 2¼"h, 2⅜"b,
$275.00 set

PLATE 433. Mug, #600 Chesterfield,
Iris Ice (crystal), 3½"w, 5⅛"h, 2¾"b, $75.00

PLATE 434. Pitcher and Tumbler, #600 Chesterfield, red, rare shape; Pitcher, 4⅝"w, 8⅝"h, 4⅛"b,
$2,000.00; Tumbler, 3⅜"w, 5¼"h, 2¼"b, $250.00

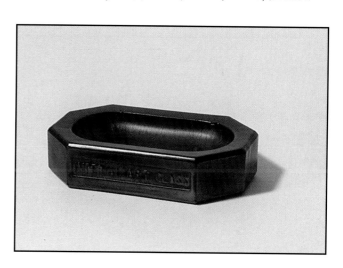

PLATE 435. Pin Tray, Imperial Art Glass
advertising, Pearl Amethyst (purple), +,
3⅛"w, 5⅜"h, 1⅛"b, rare shape, $1,200.00

PLATE 436. Lamp Shade, #561, electric, Pearl
Ruby (marigold), 3⅝"sq. w, 4½"h, 2¼"b, $65.00

PLATE 437. Lamp Shade, #575, electric,
Pearl Green (light green), 5"w, 5¼"h, 2¼"b,
$90.00

PLATE 438. Lamp Shade, #575, electric,
Peacock Iridescent (clam broth, light marigold),
4"w, 5¼"h, 2¼"b, $35.00

PLATE 439. Lamp Shade, #535, electric,
Pearl Ruby (marigold), 5"w, 4⅜"h, 2¼"b, $55.00

PLATE 440. Lamp Shade, #548, electric,
Pearl Green (light green), 5"w, 5¼"h, 2¼"b,
$70.00

PLATE 441. Lamp Shade, #544, electric,
Pearl White (crystal), 5⅛"w, 3¾"h, 2¼"b, $50.00

PLATE 442. Lamp Shade, #559, electric,
Melon-Rib, Pearl Ruby (marigold),
4½"w, 4¼"h, 2¼"b, $60.00

PLATE 443. Lamp Shade, #552, tungsten,
marked NUART, Pearl Ruby (marigold),
6½"w, 5½"h, 2¼"b, scarce shape, $130.00

PLATE 444. Lamp Shade, #594, gas,
Pearl Ruby (marigold), 6¼"w, 4⅜"h, 3¼"b, $75.00

PLATE 445. Lamp Shade, #553,
electric, marigold milk, 11⅛"w, 5½"h, 3¼"b,
rare shape, $350.00

PLATE 446. Lamp, Art Glass base and
NUART shade, Pearl Ruby (marigold),
14¼"h, $200.00

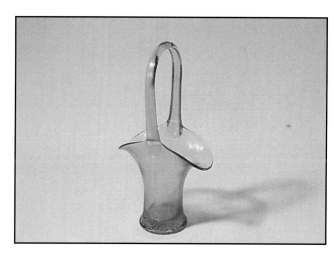

PLATE 447. Basket, #300, green,
5¾"w, 9¾"h, 3"b, rare color,
$135.00 ($75.00 marigold)

PLATE 448. Hair Receiver, #21 Art Glass,
Pearl Green (light green), 4½"w, 3¼"h, 3½"b,
$125.00

PLATE 449. Vase, Art Glass, bulb,
Pearl Silver (dark purple), 4"w, 5¼"h, 2¾"b,
$85.00

PLATE 450. Vase, #2 Art Glass, bouquet, Pearl
White (crystal), +, 8¼"w, 5"h, 2⅜"b, $115.00

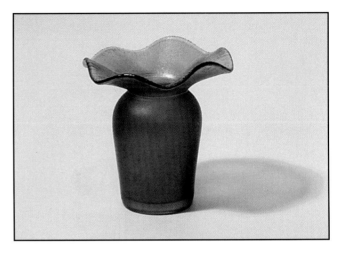

PLATE 451. Vase, #2 Art Glass, bouquet, Pearl
Green (light green), +, 5"w, 5¼"h, 2⅜"b, $125.00

PLATE 452. Vase, #6 Art Glass,
Pearl Ruby (marigold), +, 4½"w, 5⅛"h, 2⅜"b,
$90.00

PLATE 453. Vase, #30 Art Glass,
Pearl Amethyst (purple), +, 4"w, 6¼"h, 3"b
$110.00

PLATE 454. Vase, Art Glass, marigold milk,
5⅛"w, 4⅜"h, 3⅝"b, $125.00

PLATE 455. Vase, Art Glass, bulb, Pearl Ruby
(marigold), +, 3⅜"w, 6"h, 2¾"b, $125.00

PLATE 456. Vase, Art Glass, marked NUART, pearl green on emerald glass, 2¾"w, 6¼"h, 2¾"b, $150.00

PLATE 457. Vase, #692, Handkerchief Top, Iris Ice (crystal), 4"w, 4½"h, 2½"b, $40.00

PLATE 458. Vase, #692, wide flared, red, 4⅝"w, 5⅜"h, 2½"b, $100.00

PLATE 459. Vase, #692, wide flared, blue smoke milk, 4⅝"w, 5⅜"h, 2½"b, $200.00

PLATE 460. Vase, #693, wide flared, marigold milk, + inside, 6¼"w, 7⅝"h, 3½"b, $200.00

PLATE 461. Vase, #693, Rose Ice (light marigold), 6½"w, 8"h, 3½"b, $70.00

PLATE 462. Vase, #244, Grecian,
2-handled, flared, Rose Ice (light marigold),
4⅛"w, 8⅛"h, 3½"b, $90.00

PLATE 463. Vase, #244, Grecian,
2-handled, bulb shape, Blue Ice (blue smoke),
3⅛"w, 8¼"h, 3½"b, $120.00

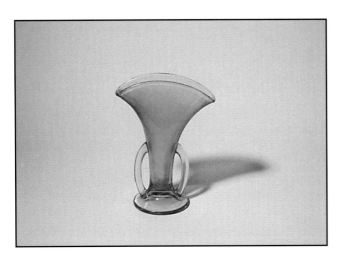

PLATE 464. Vase, #244, Grecian, 2-handled, fan,
pink marigold, 1¾" x 6⅛"w, 8⅛"h, 3½"b, $125.00

PLATE 465. Vase, #244, Grecian,
2-handled, Jack-in-the-Pulpit, Blue Ice (blue
smoke), 5"w, 7¼"h, 3½"b, $115.00

PLATE 466. Vase, #74 Art Glass,
square, Pearl Ruby (marigold), +,
9"w, 8¼"h, 3½"b, $130.00

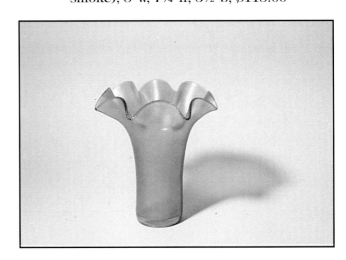

PLATE 467. Vase, #83 Art Glass, crimped,
Pearl Green (light green), +, 9¾"w, 10⅜"h, 3½"b,
$160.00

PLATE 468. Vase, #693, Amethyst Ice (purple),
5¼"w, 10¾"h, 3½"b, $100.00

PLATE 469. Vase, #693, Blue Ice (blue smoke),
5¾"w, 10¾"h, 3½"b, $70.00

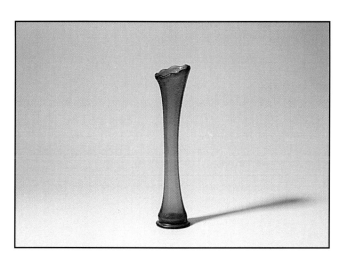

PLATE 470. Vase, #692, bud, Green Ice
(blue-green), 2¼"w, 11¼"h, 2½"b, $75.00

PLATE 471. Vase, Green Ice (blue-green),
7"w, 12¼"h, 4⅜"b, $150.00

PLATE 472. Vase, Blue Ice (blue smoke),
9"w, 16¼"h, 5⅜"b, $175.00

PLATE 473. Vase, red, 7½"w, 17"h, 5⅜"b,
$800.00

JEANNETTE GLASS COMPANY

Jeannette, Pennsylvania

Jeannette Glass Co., Jeannette, Pennsylvania, made little stretch glass but the company produced some common bowls with outstanding gold iridescence. Though best known for their popular depression glass patterns (e.g., Cherry Blossom, Doric, Swirl, and Iris) and opaque colors (e.g., Delphite, Jadite, and Shell Pink), they commonly iridized pieces in the 1920s and 1930s. Some of these were heavily iridized and given the stretch effect. The actual name given to their stretch glass has been difficult to confidently identify, but Sunset line has been found. In advertisements, they often used sunset and satin effect, rainbow and golden iridescent. The following colors are known:

Gold – crystal glass with bright gold iridescence, commonly with light green to purple overtones – a light marigold (Plate 475.)

Amber – crystal glass with amber iridescence – a richer marigold; Jeannette also used Topaz to describe some noniridized glass which was a true amber light brown glass (Plate 477.)

Purple – a medium purple glass, often with faint swirls of darker color (Plate 480.)

Green – an olive-green (light green-yellow) glass, not like the lighter Florentine Green of Fenton (Plate 481).

White – crystal glass with white iridescence (not illustrated).

blue – light blue glass with slight green overtones (not illustrated).

The most common Jeannette piece is the large 12" bowl with gold colored stretch. This bowl almost always has excellent stretch marks and intense iridescence ranging from bright gold to gold with purple to green accents. Amber and White pieces are less common with Purple, Green, and blue pieces being rare.

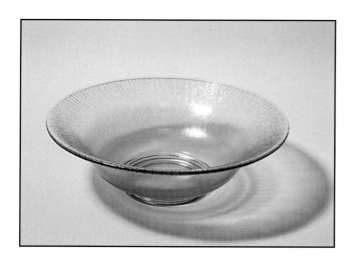

PLATE 474. Bowl, flared, collar base, Gold (light marigold), 12"w, 3¾"h, 4⅝"b, $55.00

PLATE 475. Bowl, flared, ground base, Gold (light marigold), 12¼"w, 3¼"h, 3"b, $55.00

PLATE 476. Bowl, flared, Gold (light marigold), 10"w, 3¼"h, 4⅝"b, $40.00

PLATE 477. Bowl, flared, 3-footed base, Amber (marigold), 10"w, 3¾"h, 4½"b, $40.00

PLATE 478. Bowl, flared, 3-footed base, Amber (marigold), 9"w, 3"h, 2⅞"b, $45.00

PLATE 479. Bowl, flared, 3-footed base, Gold (light marigold), 9⅛"w, 3"h, 2⅞"b, $45.00

PLATE 480. Bowl, footed, flared,
Purple (light purple), 9⅜"w, 3½"h, 3⅞"b, $90.00

PLATE 481. Bowl, footed, flared, crimped,
Green, 8½"w, 4⅛"h, 4"b, $80.00

PLATE 482. Server, wide shovel handled, Amber
(marigold), 9¾"w, 4½"h, 3¼"b, $55.00

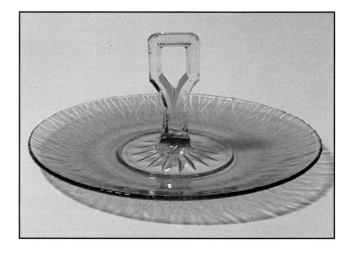

PLATE 483. Server, narrow shovel handled,
impressed star, Amber (marigold), 10"w, 4½"h,
$50.00

LANCASTER GLASS COMPANY

Lancaster, Ohio

Lancaster Glass Co., Lancaster, Ohio, began making glasswares in 1908 and by the 1920s had joined other companies in making tableware that was iridized. In 1924, they came under control of the Hocking Glass Company but production continued under their own name until 1937. In the 1920s, they produced a line referred to as Lustre which can be identified as stretch glass. In advertisements the terms "luster (sic) glass" and "lustres" are used. The following terms have been identified as referring to stretch glass colors:

Aztec – crystal glass with yellow-gold iridescence, a bright marigold (Plate 484).
Ruby Lustre – crystal glass with white iridescence and the glass with red to orange enamel fired onto the underside (Plate 497).
green lustre – like Ruby Lustre but with green to yellow enamel (Plate 501).
white lustre – like Ruby Lustre but with cream to white enamel (Plate 485).
Iris Ice – crystal glass with white iridescence (Plate 491).
Rose Ice – crystal glass with red-orange iridescence, a red-orange marigold (Plate 487).
pink – a pink glass with light iridescence, color name not identified (Plate 504).

Lancaster's Lustres in Ruby, green, and white are moderately common and easily identified because of the enamel and flower decorations. Iris Ice and Aztec pieces are also fairly common, especially in covered pieces. The Rose Ice is probably less common and the iridescence can be damaged with improper cleaning. The pink is also fairly uncommon and can be confused with some of Imperial's pink pieces.

PLATE 484. Bowl, flared, Aztec (marigold), 10"w, 2¾"h, 4"b, $45.00

PLATE 485. Bowl, flared, white lustre, (crystal) with white enamel, 9⅞"w, 3"h, 4"b, $60.00

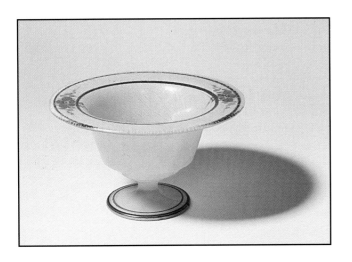

PLATE 486. Comport, flared, flattened, white lustre (crystal) with white enamel, 7⅛"w, 4"h, 3⅛"b, $50.00

PLATE 487. Comport, flared, Rose Ice (dark marigold-brown), 8¾"w, 4⅞"h, 4¼"b, $90.00

PLATE 488. Comport, flared, white lustre, (crystal) with white enamel, 9"w, 4¾"h, 4¼"b, $75.00

PLATE 489. Comport, flared, round stem, Aztec (marigold), 7⅜"w, 5⅜"h, 3⅜"b, $60.00

PLATE 490. Comport, flared, flattened, six-sided stem, Aztec (marigold), 8"w, 4¼"h, 3½"b, $40.00

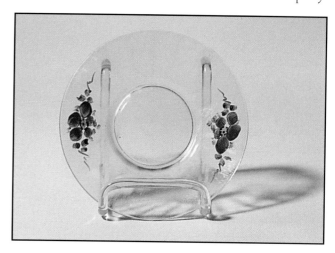

PLATE 491. Plate, Iris Ice (crystal) with decoration, 6¼"w, 2⅞"b, $20.00

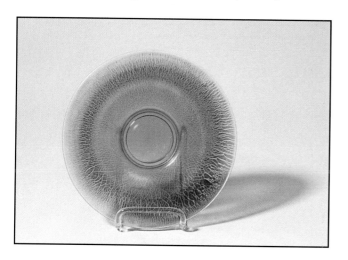

PLATE 492. Plate, Rose Ice (dark marigold-brown), 9"w, 3"b, $40.00

PLATE 493. Server, shovel handled, Rose Ice (dark marigold-brown), 11"w, 4¾"h, 3¾"b, $70.00

PLATE 494. Server, shovel handled, Iris Ice (crystal) with decoration, 11"w, 4½"h, 4"b, $50.00

PLATE 495. Cheese and Cracker Set, Aztec (marigold); Cheese Dish, 5⅜"w, 2¾"h, 3"b; Plate, ground foot, 9⅞"w, 5½"h, $65.00 set

PLATE 496. Cheese and Cracker Set,
Iris Ice (crystal) with decoration; Cheese Dish,
5"w, 3⅜"h, 3b; Plate, 4"w, 3"b, $90.00 set

PLATE 497. Bonbon, covered,
Ruby Lustre (crystal) with red-orange enamel,
6¼"w, 5⅜"h, 3"b, $70.00

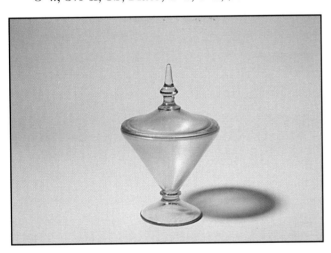

PLATE 498. Candy Jar, covered, Iris Ice
(crystal), 5¼"w, 8"h, 3¼"b, $40.00

PLATE 499. Candy Jars, covered,
white lustre (crystal) with white enamel;
Short Footed, 5¼"w, 6½"h, 3¼"b, $65.00;
Tall Footed, 5¼"w, 8¾"h, 3¼"b, $85.00

PLATE 500. Candy Jar, covered,
three-footed, optic rays, Iris Ice (crystal),
7⅛"w, 4⅛"b, $95.00 with lid

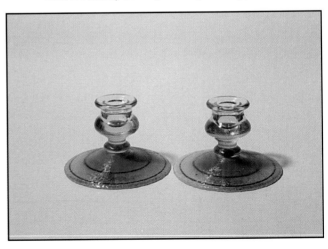

PLATE 501. Candlesticks, green lustre
(crystal) with green enamel, 1⅞"w, 3¼"h, 5"b,
$80.00

PLATE 502. Mayonnaise, flared, flattened, Aztec (marigold), 6½"w, 4¼"h, 3⅝"b, rare shape, $80.00

PLATE 503. Server, cake, footed, Rose Ice (dark marigold), 11"w, 2¼"h, 4¼"b, $90.00

PLATE 504. Server, cake, footed, pink with satin and paint decoration, 11"w, 2½"h, 4¼"b, rare color, $125.00

PLATE 505. Vase, rolled, flared, Sweet Pea, Rose Ice (dark marigold), 8¾"w, 5½"h, 3⅝"b, $75.00

H. NORTHWOOD & COMPANY

Wheeling, West Virginia

H. Northwood & Co., Wheeling, West Virginia, was one of the major producers of stretch glass from 1916 to their demise in 1925. Fortunately, Harry Northwood was a master salesman, and numerous industry references and advertisements exist to help identify their stretch glass lines, colors, and pieces. As stated in Heacock, Measell and Wiggins' book on Northwood (1991), Northwood usually used the name "Rainbow Line" when referring to stretch glass. However, the terms "Satin Sheen" and "Cobweb" were also used to refer to their stretch glass. Industry publications and advertisements often used the following descriptive terms: cobweb, iridescent, satin sheen, and iris. Most of Northwood's colors have been identified but there are numerous pieces known to us for which we have not been able find a color name. The colors known to us are:

Blue – common blue glass, like Fenton's Celeste Blue (Plate 521).
dark blue – a darker blue glass than the Blue above; this may simply be a batch difference, but there are enough pieces to clearly determine that these two distinct colors exist in quantity (Plate 511).
blue-green – a light blue-green glass, close to the Blue but with a definite greenish cast; this may simply be a batch difference, but there are enough pieces to warrant a different color name (Plate 562).
dark green – a dark, emerald-green glass which does not seem to have been given a specific name (Plate 514).
Ivory – opaque white-yellow or custard-white glass with light iridescence (Plate 513).
Jade Blue – opaque light blue-green glass with light iridescence; color can vary considerably from light sky-blue to deeper blue-green (Plate 508).
marigold – crystal glass with typical orange-gold, 'marigold' iridescence; not specifically identified in advertisements containing the Rainbow and Cobweb lines but referred to as Golden Iris in their carnival lines (Plate 512).
opaque white – opaque white glass, a milk glass, with light iridescence (Plate 542).
Pearl – crystal glass with white iridescence (Plate 558).
Royal Purple – violet, a medium blue-purple glass (Plate 563).
Russet – a green-brown-yellow glass or olive-amber color; not amber or olive-green (Plate 506).
Sateena – a dark amber glass, not a dark Russet (not illustrated).
Topaz – yellow-green glass; commonly called vaseline (Plate 523).

Blue, Topaz, Russet, and Jade Blue are the most common Northwood colors. Dark green, marigold, Royal Purple, and Pearl are less common. Ivory or custard pieces are also uncommon. Only a few pieces of the Sateena and opaque white are known. Though fairly common, the Jade Blue is a highly desirable color, especially when well iridized. Though Fenton and Cambridge made a similar opaque blue glass, Northwood is the only company known to have iridized and stretched this glass. Because of the uniqueness of Jade Blue, Ivory, and Russet, many pieces of glass have been attributed to Northwood after a piece was found in one of these unique colors.

Russet is a color that is commonly mistaken for amber and olive-green colored glass that was made by Fenton, Imperial, U.S. Glass, and Vineland. However, if you compare Russet with the other glass pieces, side-by-side, they will be clearly different in color.

PLATE 506. Bowl, #301, raised, sided, Russet, 4½"w, 2¼"h, 2⅜"b, $25.00

PLATE 507. Bowl, #670, cupped, Russet, 4⅝"w, 2¼"h, 3¼"b, $40.00

PLATE 508. Bowl, #672, flared, Jade Blue, 5¼"w, 2¼"h, 3¼"b, scarce shape, $60.00

PLATE 509. Bowl, #638, cupped, 27 ribs, Jade Blue, 6½"w, 2½"h, 3½"b, $50.00

PLATE 510. Bowl, #638, flared, cupped, 27 ribs, Pearl (crystal with marigold highlight), 8⅜"w, 2"h, 3½"b, $45.00

PLATE 511. Bowl, #640, cupped, dark blue, 5⅝"w, 3⅜"h, 2½"b, $30.00

PLATE 512. Bowl, #641, wide, cupped,
marigold, 7⅞"w, 2"h, 2½"b, $35.00

PLATE 513. Bowl, #641, wide cupped,
Ivory (custard) with black trim, 8⅜"w, 2"h, 2⅜"b,
rare color, $125.00 ($35.00 blue)

PLATE 514. Bowl, #642, rolled rim, dark green,
7⅛"w, 2½"h, 2½"b, scarce color, $70.00
($35.00 blue)

PLATE 515. Bowl, #650, Baked Apple,
wide flared, Jade Blue, 6⅝"w, 1½"h, 2½"b,
scarce color, $60.00 ($40.00 blue)

PLATE 516. Bowl, #650, Russet with silver
plated handle and fork, 6⅞"w, 1¾"h, 2½"b,
$75.00 set

PLATE 517. Bowl, #650, Topaz with wheel
cutting, 6⅞"w, 1½"h, 2½"b, scarce decoration,
$60.00

PLATE 518. Bowl, #669, flared, Russet,
8"w, 3¼"h, 4⅜"b, $50.00 ($40.00 blue)

PLATE 519. Bowl, #620, flared, Jade Blue
with ground marie, 8½"w, 3½"h, 5"b, $70.00

PLATE 520. Bowl, #662, cupped, 28 optic rays,
Russet, 7⅝"w, 3½"h, 3⅞"b, $65.00

PLATE 521. Bowl, #717, wide cupped,
Blue, 12½"w, 2⅝"h, 3⅜"b, $65.00

PLATE 522. Bowl, flared, optic swirl,
Blue, 11¾"w, 3¼"h, 3½"b, scarce shape, $125.00

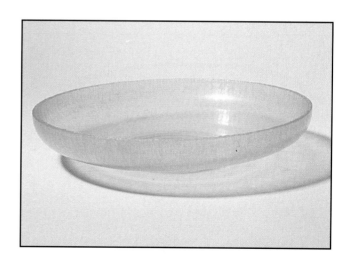

PLATE 523. Bowl, wide cupped,
ground foot, Topaz, 10¾"w, 2"h, 4"b, $60.00

PLATE 524. Bowl, ground foot, dark green, 10½"w, 2⅛"h, 3⅞"b, scarce color, $100.00

PLATE 525. Bowl, #648, wide flared, Blue, 12"w, 3⅝"h, 3½"b, $60.00

PLATE 526. Bowl, #692, flared-straight sided, Russet, 9½"w, 3¼"h, 2½"b, $65.00

PLATE 527. Bowl, #692, flared, with handles, Topaz with silver plated rim, 8"w, 2½"h, 2⅜"b, $90.00

PLATE 528. Bowl, #693, flared, cupped, marigold, 7¾"w, 4"h, 2½"b, $50.00

PLATE 529. Bowl, #694, rolled rim, Blue, 8⅞"w, 3⅜"h, 2⅝"b, $45.00

PLATE 530. Bowl, #663, flared, 28 optic rays, Ivory (custard), 9⅝"w, 3¼"h, 4"b, scarce color, $130.00

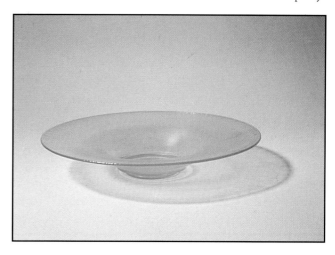

PLATE 531. Bowl, #648, wide flared, Topaz, 13½"w, 2⅜"h, 3⅝"b, $75.00

PLATE 532. Bowl, #673, flared, Russet with gold trim, 11¾"w, 3½"h, 3½"b, $75.00

PLATE 533. Bowl and Stand Set; Bowl, #673, flared, Blue, 11¾"w, 3½"h, 3½"b, $60.00; Stand, #709, tall, opaque black not iridized, 4⅝"w, 3½"h, 5⅞"b, rare stand shape, $100.00

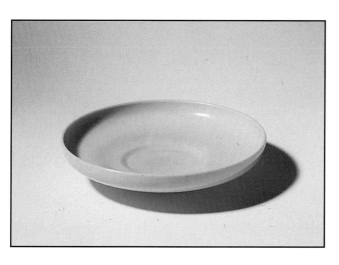

PLATE 534. Bowl, #616, wide flared, cupped, Ivory (custard), 10⅝"w, 2¼"h, 3⅞"b, scarce color, $125.00

PLATE 535. Bowl, #697, flared, cupped, Russet, 9¾"w, 4½"h, 3⅜"b, $55.00

PLATE 536. Bowl, #649, rolled rim,
Russet, 11½"w, 3⅛"h, 3½"b, $60.00

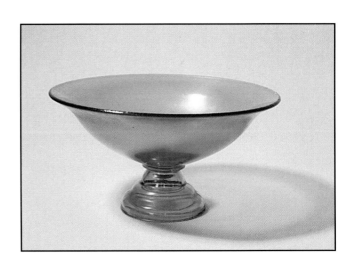

PLATE 537. Bowl, #721, attached 3-ring foot,
Blue, 10⅝"w, 5½"h, 4"b, only one known, $250.00

PLATE 538. Bowl, #713, footed, flared,
Russet, 9⅞"w, 5⅛"h, 4⅝"b, $70.00

PLATE 539. Bowl, #715, footed, rolled rim,
Russet, 10¼"w, 4"h, 4⅝"b, $70.00

PLATE 540. Bowl, #677, footed, flared,
Russet, 11½"w, 4⅞"h, 5⅛"b, $100.00

PLATE 541. Bowl, #678, black footed, flared,
28 optic rays, Blue, 11¾"w, 4¾"h, 5⅛"b, $125.00

PLATE 542. Bowl, #678, black footed, flared,
28 optic rays, opaque white, 12"w, 4½"h, 5⅛"b,
only two known, $1,000.00

PLATE 543. Bowl, #679, black footed,
flared, cupped, Jade Blue, 10½"w, 5¼"h, 5¼"b,
$200.00

PLATE 544. Bowl, #681, black footed,
cupped, Blue, 9"w, 5¾"h, 5¼"b, $125.00

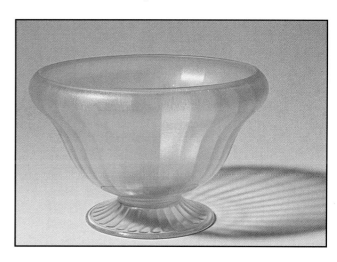

PLATE 545. Bowl, #682, footed, cupped,
28 optic rays, Topaz, 9¼"w, 5¾"h, 5⅛"b, $130.00

PLATE 546. Bowl, #684, footed, rolled rim,
28 optic rays, Blue, 11¾"w, 4¼"h, 5¼"b, $130.00

PLATE 547. Bowl, #707, fern, 3-footed,
cupped, rib optic, Russet, 4½"w, 2¾"h, 1¾"b,
$75.00

117

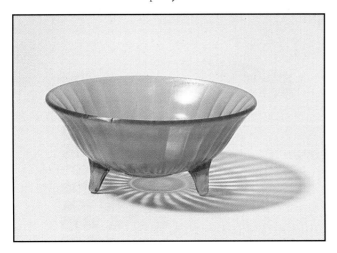

PLATE 548. Bowl, #707, fern, 3-footed, flared, rib optic, Blue, 6⅛"w, 2½"h, 1¾"b, $60.00

PLATE 549. Comport, #652, flared, dark blue, 7¼"w, 4"h, 3"b, $35.00

PLATE 550. Comport, #653, wide flared, cupped, Topaz with gold trim, 8⅜"w, 2¾"h, 3"b, $50.00

PLATE 551. Comport, #654, flared straight side, Russet, 8⅝"w, 3¾"h, 3"b, $45.00

PLATE 552. Comport, #656, flared, cupped, Russet, 7½"w, 3"h, 3⅛"b, $50.00

PLATE 553. Comport, #644, cupped Rose Bowl, 15 panels, Jade Blue, 5"w, 3½"h, 3½"b, $60.00

PLATE 554. Comport, #645, wide flared, cupped, 15 panels, Jade Blue, 6½"w, 3"h, 3½"b, $50.00

PLATE 555. Comport, #646, flattened Card Tray, Russet, 7⅛"w, 2½"h, 3½"b, $50.00

PLATE 556. Comport, cupped, octagonal foot with no tree bark, Topaz, 4⅝"w, 3⅝"h, 3⅛"b, $45.00

PLATE 557. Comport, cupped, octagonal foot with tree bark, dark blue, 4⅝"w, 3½"h, 3⅛"b, $50.00

PLATE 558. Comport, #605, wide flared, cupped, square foot with tree bark, Pearl (crystal), 8½"w, 2½"h, 3"b, $60.00

PLATE 559. Comport, #609, rolled rim, square foot with tree bark, dark green, 8⅛"w, 3¼"h, 3"b, scarce color, $90.00

PLATE 560. Comport, #807, cupped, square
foot with tree bark, dark green, 6½"w, 3⅞"h, 3"b,
scarce color, $90.00

PLATE 561. Comport, cupped rose bowl,
square foot with tree bark, Blue, 5⅜"w, 4"h, 3"b,
rare shape, $75.00

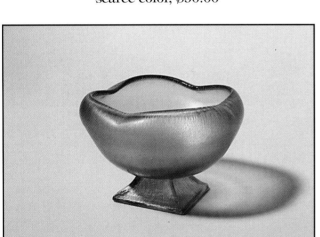

PLATE 562. Comport, #807, cupped, crimped,
square foot with tree bark, light blue-green,
6"w, 4"h, 3"b, scarce color, $95.00

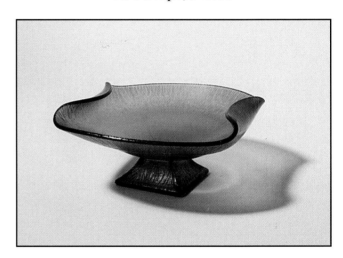

PLATE 563. Comport, #605, wide flared, 2-sides
cupped, square foot with tree bark, Royal Purple
(violet), 9" x 6¾"w, 3"h, 3"b, scarce color, $75.00

PLATE 564. Comport, #605, Jack-in-the-Pulpit,
square foot with tree bark, Blue,
8½"w, 1¾ -4¼"h, 3"b, $65.00

PLATE 565. Comport, wide flared,
12-sided foot, no tree bark, Topaz,
9½"w, 5⅛"h, 4½"b, scarce foot, $100.00

PLATE 566. Comport, wide flared,
12-sided foot with tree bark, Topaz,
9¼"w, 5⅛"h, 4½"b, $90.00

PLATE 567. Comport, wide cupped,
12-sided foot with tree bark, "N" mark,
Blue, 7¾"w, 5½"h, 4⅝"b, signed, $90.00

PLATE 568. Comport, flattened cake stand,
12-sided foot with tree bark, marigold, 10½"w,
4⅜"h, 4½"b, rare shape/color, $100.00

PLATE 569. Comport, #637, flared, cupped, no
ribs, Topaz, 5¾"w, 6¾"h, 3⅜"b, rare shape,
$85.00

PLATE 570. Comport, #637, flared bell shape,
21 ribs, Jade Blue, 5¾"w, 7"h, 3⅜"b,
$90.00 ($65.00 blue)

PLATE 571. Comport, #637, flared rolled rim,
21 ribs, Jade Blue, 5⅞"w, 6"h, 3⅜"b, $90.00

PLATE 572. Comport, #637, flared, cupped, 21 ribs, dark green, 5½"w, 7"h, 3⅜"b, scarce color, $150.00

PLATE 573. Comport, #637, flared, flat rim, 21 ribs, Blue, 7⅞"w, 5¾"h, 3⅜"b, $65.00

PLATE 574. Comport, #637, nearly flat, 21 ribs, Topaz, 8⅜"w, 5"h, 3⅜"b, scarce shape, $125.00

PLATE 575. Comport, #666, wide flared, cupped, Russet, 7¾"w, 6¾"h, 4¼"b, scarce shape, $100.00

PLATE 576. Comport, #705, flared, 6-sided stem with two balls, Topaz, 6⅝"w, 7½"h, 3½"b, $65.00

PLATE 577. Sherbet, #685, flared, plain, Russet, 4¼"w, 3½"h, 2¾"b, $40.00

PLATE 578. Sherbet and Under-Plate Set,
Blue with gold trim, $70.00 set; Sherbet, #685,
flared, plain, 4"w, 3½"h, 2¾"b, $25.00;
Plate, #729, 8"w, 5½"b, $45.00

PLATE 579. Sherbet flared, eight panels, Russet
with gold trim, 3¾"w, 3½"h, 2¾"b, $65.00

PLATE 580. Custard/Ice Cream and Under-Plate
Set, #722, Blue; Custard/Ice Cream, straight
sided flared, 3¼"w, 1⅞"h, 1¾"b;
Plate, ground foot, 8"w, 5½"b, $60.00 set

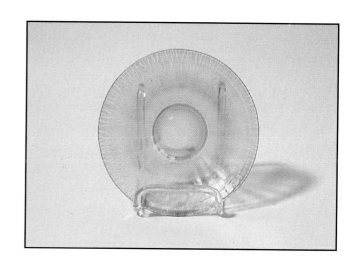

PLATE 581. Plate #301, 20 optic rays,
Blue, 6½"w, 2¼"b, $20.00

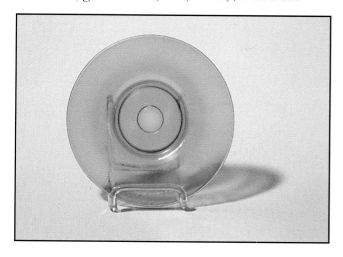

PLATE 582. Plate #622, with ground marie,
Blue, 7¾"w, 3⅜"b, $30.00

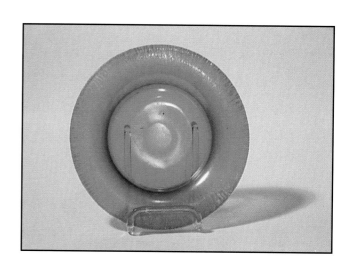

PLATE 583. Plate #630, with ground marie,
dark blue, 8¾"w, 5¼"b, $30.00

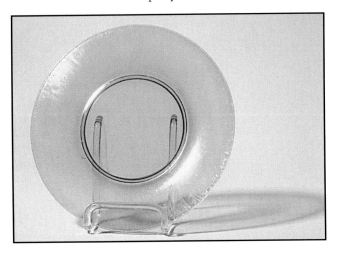

PLATE 584. Plate, ground foot,
Russet, 9"w, 4¾"b, $40.00

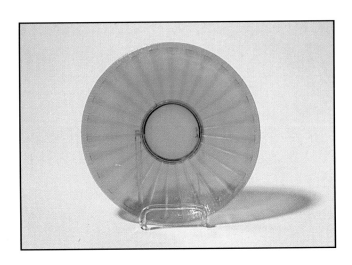

PLATE 585. Plate #639, 27 ribs,
Blue, 9½"w, 3½"b, $45.00

PLATE 586. Plate #631, 28 optic rays,
Jade Blue, 11¾"w, 4"b, $75.00

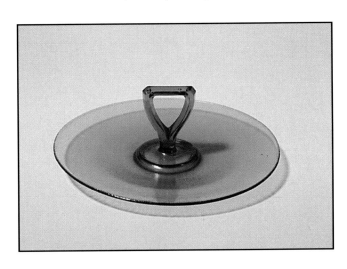

PLATE 587. Server, #698, handled,
Blue, 11"w, 4"h, 3"b, $50.00

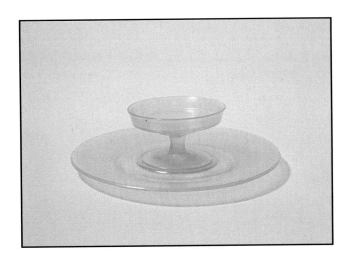

PLATE 588. Cheese and Cracker Set, #699,
Topaz; Cheese Dish, 4⅝"w, 2½"h, 3¼"b;
Plate, ground foot, 9⅞"w, 5¾"b, $75.00 set

PLATE 589. Candy Jar, #707 with lid, 3-footed,
Topaz, 4⅝"w, 5"h, 1¾"b, rare with lid, $150.00

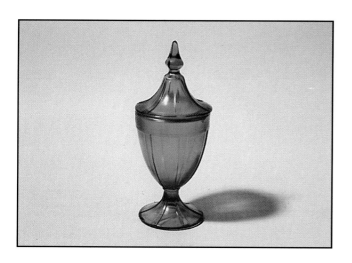

PLATE 590. Candy Jar, #659, ½-lb,
Blue, 3⅞"w, 9¼"h, 3½"b, $55.00

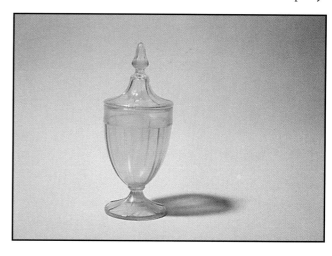

PLATE 591. Candy Jar, #636, 1-lb,
Topaz, 4¼"w, 10"h, 3⅞"b, $65.00

PLATE 592. Bonbon, #643, covered,
Blue, 5⅜"w, 6"h, 3½"b, $45.00

PLATE 593. Bonbon, #643, covered,
Ivory (custard), 5⅜"w, 6"h, 3⅝"b,
scarce color, $175.00

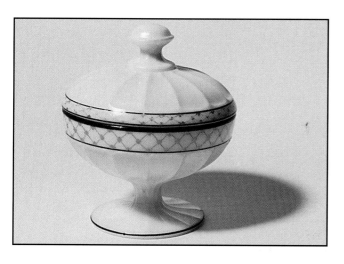

PLATE 594. Bonbon, #643, covered,
opaque white with black and gold decoration,
5"w, 6"h, 3"b, only one known, $500.00

PLATE 595. Candlesticks, #676,
Jade Blue, 2⅝"h, 4⅝"b, $100.00 pair

PLATE 596. Candlestick, #675, handled,
Russet, 3"h, 3"b, $120.00 pair

PLATE 597. Candlesticks, Trumpet Twist, Blue,
6⅜"h, 3⅞"b, scarce shape, $110.00 pair

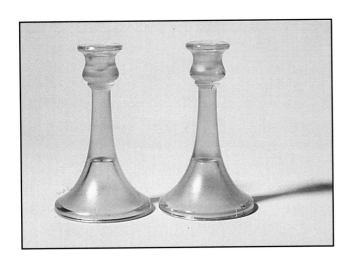

PLATE 598. Candlesticks, #719, Trumpet,
Topaz, 6½"h, 3⅞"b, $75.00 pair

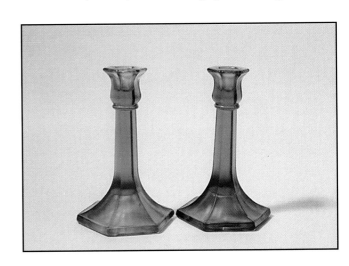

PLATE 599. Candlesticks, #658, 6-sided,
Blue, 6⅞"h, 4"b, $75.00 pair

PLATE 600. Candlesticks, #657, 6-sided, Ivory
(custard), 8½"h, 4⅜"b, scarce color, $150.00 pair
($85.00 blue)

PLATE 601. Candlesticks, #695, Colonial,
6-sided, Russet, 8¾"h, 3⅞"b, $120.00 pair
($90.00 blue)

PLATE 602. Candlesticks, #696, Colonial,
6-sided, Blue, 10¼"h, 4⅛"b, $130.00 pair

PLATE 603. Candlesticks, #708, Spindle,
Blue, 8¾"h, 4½"b, scarce shape, $120.00 pair

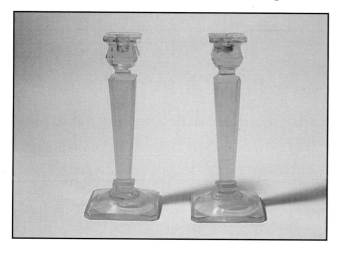

PLATE 604. Candlesticks, #651, 4-sided,
Topaz, 11"h, 4½"b, $200.00 pair

PLATE 605. Night Set #559, Russet, $400.00 set;
Pitcher, diamond optic, 2⅞"w, 6½"h, 4⅛"b,
$300.00; Tumbler, diamond pattern, 2½"w, 3½"h,
2⅞"b, $100.00

PLATE 606. Night Set, #559, diamond optic, Jade
Blue, rare color, $800.00 set; Pitcher, diamond
optic, 2⅞"w, 6½"h, 4⅛"b, $600.00; Tumbler, dia-
mond pattern, 2½"w, 3½"h, 2⅞"b, $200.00

PLATE 607. Tumbler, #700, optic panels,
Topaz, 2¾"w, 3⅞"h, 2½"b, scarce shape, $150.00

PLATE 608. Tumbler, #688, handled, optic panels, Blue, 3¼"w, 4⅝"h, 2¼"b, only two known, $250.00

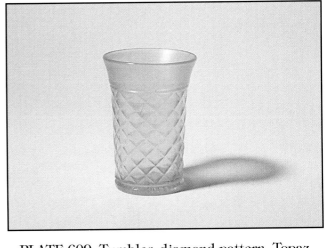

PLATE 609. Tumbler, diamond pattern, Topaz, 3¼"w, 4⅝"h, 2⅜"b, scarce color, $120.00

PLATE 610. Pitcher and Tumbler Set, 10 pieces with coasters, Blue, $430.00 set; Pitcher, covered, diamond optic, 4"w, 11¾"h, 4⅝"b, $250.00; Tumblers, diamond pattern, 3¼"w, 4⅝"h, 2⅜"b, $30.00 each; Coasters, #5, cobalt not iridized, 3¼"w, ⅜"h, $15.00 each

PLATE 611. Cream and Sugar Set, optic rays, Topaz, only known set; Creamer, 3¾"w, 4¼"h, 2½"b, $100.00; Sugar missing lid, 4¼"w, 3⅞"h, 2⅞"b, $100.00

PLATE 612. Sugar, covered, optic rays, Topaz, 4⅛"w, 6"h, 2⅞"b, rare shape, $125.00

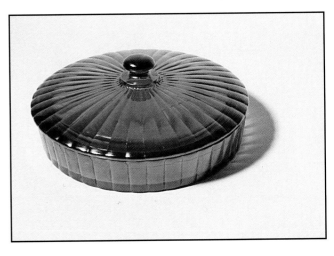

PLATE 613. Almond or Bonbon, #691, covered, Russet, 6½"w, 2½"h, 6⅛"b, $75.00

PLATE 614. Nut Cup, with 8 panels,
"N" mark, Blue, 3"w, 1⅝"h, 2⅛", scarce shape,
$75.00

PLATE 615. Mayonnaise, #704, flattened rim,
Blue, 6⅜"w, 4"h, 3½"b, $40.00

PLATE 616. Mayonnaise and Under-Plate Set,
Topaz, $50.00 set; Bowl, #621, flared,
ground marie, 5¼"w, 2⅝"h, 2⅞"b, $30.00;
Plate, #674, ground marie, 7⅝"w, 3½"b, $20.00

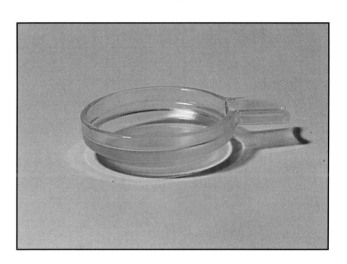

PLATE 617. Ash Tray, #723, Topaz,
3½"w, 1"h, 1¾"b, $50.00

PLATE 618. Ash Tray, #706, and Fern Bowl, #707
Set, Blue, 4⅞"w, 3½"h, 1¾"b, rare set, $150.00

PLATE 619. Candlestick/Lamp, #651,
electrified, Blue, 2¼"w, 11"h, 4½"b, $300.00

PLATE 620. Lamp Shade, ribbed, flared,
marigold milk, 5"w, 5"h, 2⅛"b, $65.00

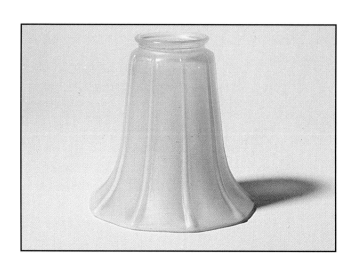

PLATE 621. Lamp Shade, ribbed, flared,
opaque white, 5"w, 5"h, 2⅛"b, $65.00

PLATE 622. Vase, #569, flared, flat rim,
rib optic, Blue, 5⅜"w, 4½"h, 3⅛"b, $75.00

PLATE 623. Vase, #569, flared, crimped, rib
optic, Royal Purple (violet), 6"w, 5¼"h, 3⅛"b,
$110.00

PLATE 624. Vase, flared rolled rim,
rib optic, Blue, 8"w, 7¼"h, 4"b, $100.00

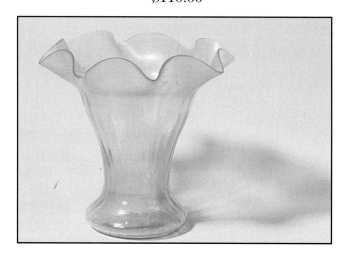

PLATE 625. Vase, flared, crimped,
rib optic, Topaz, 8½"w, 8"h, 4"b, $150.00

PLATE 626. Vase, wide flat rim, ground foot,
Pearl (crystal), 8"w, 4¼"h, 2½"b, $85.00

PLATE 627. Vase, wide rolled rim,
ground foot, Royal Purple (violet),
6½"w, 3⅞"h, 2¾"b, rare shape/color, $90.00

PLATE 628. Vase, flared, crimped,
ground foot, Royal Purple (violet),
5⅜"w, 6⅛"h, 2¾"b, rare shape/color, $90.00

PLATE 629. Vase, flared, ground foot,
Jade Blue, 8½"w, 7¾"h, 3⅜"b, $150.00

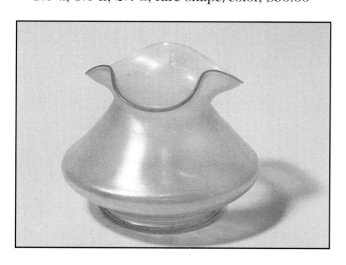

PLATE 630. Vase, crimped,
Pearl (crystal), 5¼"w, 5½"h, 4⅛"b, $65.00

PLATE 631. Vase, #618, flared, rib optic,
Blue, 4"w, 6"h, 4⅛"b, $75.00

PLATE 632. Vase, #618, flared, diamond optic,
Jade Blue, 4½"w, 6⅛"h, 4⅛"b, rare color, $250.00

PLATE 633. Vase, #613, flared crimped,
diamond optic, Blue, 5½"w, 6"h, 4⅛"b, $75.00

PLATE 634. Vase, cupped rim, Royal
Purple (violet), 3⅛"w, 6¼"h, 4⅛"b,
scarce color, $95.00

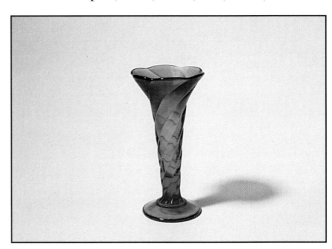

PLATE 635. Vase, #727, twist, short,
Blue, 3½"w, 7⅛"h, 3"b, $70.00

PLATE 636. Vase, #727,
twist, tall, Blue,
3¾"w, 9½"h, 3⅜"b, $70.00

PLATE 637. Vase, #989,
swung Four Pillar, Russet,
4"w, 11⅝"h, 4"b, $50.00

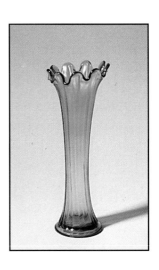

PLATE 638. Vase, #816,
swung Fine Rib, Russet,
4"w, 11½"h, 3⅜"b, $50.00

UNITED STATES GLASS COMPANY

Pittsburgh, Pennsylvania

FACTORY K – KING GLASS
Pittsburgh, Pennsylvania

FACTORY R – TIFFIN GLASS
Tiffin, Ohio

The United States Glass Co., Pittsburgh, Pennsylvania, was formed in 1891 by joining 15 American glass manufacturers. Among these original companies was the King Glass Co., Pittsburgh, which was designated as Factory K. In 1892, the A.J. Beatty & Sons, Tiffin, Ohio, plant joined the company as Factory R and was later known as Tiffin Glass Co. As with most companies within the U.S. Glass consortium, King Glass and Tiffin Glass appeared to operate independently of each other though there is considerable evidence that molds may have been shared or, at least, very similar designs were made in their factories. At the writing of this book, there is ample evidence that the Tiffin factory made many pieces of satin glass and some pearl-iridized (simple, shiny, white iridescence) pieces. The King factory apparently made most, if not all, of what we would call stretch glass. However, in our opinion, we believe that both factories were involved in making stretch glass.

In the U.S. Glass advertisements where stretch glass is illustrated, the term "Aurora" is used and must refer to the stretch effect. The term "Aurora effect" was associated with numerous other lines including Autumn, Carrara, Cumula, Florentine, Pomona, 15,151 line, 15,189 line, 15,310 line, and 15,314 line. The following colors of U.S. Glass stretch glass are known to us:

amber – a true amber, a yellow-orange to yellow-brown glass; not listed in any known advertisements or industry journals (Plate 661).

black amethyst – a very dark purple glass with multicolored iridescence; not listed (Plate 698).

Blue – a medium blue glass, like Celeste Blue of Fenton (Plate 639).

Canary and Topaz – yellow-green glass; commonly called vaseline by modern collectors (Plate 653).

Coral – an opaque orange to yellow-orange slag glass in the Carrara Line; often called salmon by stretch glass collectors (Plate 700).

Crystal – crystal glass with white iridescence (Plate 673).

Green – a normal green glass, like Florentine Green of Fenton (Plate 646).

light blue-green – a very light blue-green, almost like Fenton's Aquamarine (Plate 642).

Jade and Jade Green – a translucent to opaque green glass; ranges from true jade green to a blue-green color (Plate 690).

Royal Blue – a light cobalt blue transparent glass, often called Tiffin Blue by Tiffin collectors (Plate 684).

Mandarin Yellow – a translucent to opaque yellow glass; this may not actually be the name of the opaque yellow since some Tiffin advertisements refer to a Mandarin color which appears to be a transparent yellow-amber glass (Plate 689).

Nile Green – an opaque green slag glass with white iridescence; the slag mix contains light green with emerald green spots and swirls; part of the Carrara Line (Plate 650).

Old Rose – a translucent to opaque pink glass with iridescence; occasionally brownish or caramel in color, possibly from improper heating of the heat-sensitive colorants; color name may actually refer to transparent glass but is currently considered part of the Carrara Line (Plate 671.).

olive green – an olive-green glass, not listed by U.S. Glass; commonly confused with Northwood's Russet (Plate 666).

Pearl Blue – an opaque light blue slag glass with light iridescence (Plate 643).

Pearl Gray – an opaque cream with tan to dark brown slag glass with light iridescence (Plate 640).

Pink – light pink glass, like Velva Rose of Fenton (Plate 644).

red slag – a translucent to opaque red slag glass, more of a pigeon blood red than the yellow-orange of Coral; not listed in advertisements (Plate 728).
light purple – a light purple glass, commonly called wisteria, not listed in advertisements (Plate 662).

Blue, Topaz, Crystal, and Pink are probably the most common U.S. Glass colors, though the amber and olive green are fairly easy to find. The Royal Blue, light purple, and black amethyst colors are much more difficult to find and these are desirable colors.

U.S. Glass made some of the most interesting translucent and opaque stretch glass. Most beginning collectors pass up these pieces because the iridescence is often very delicate and the piece must be held in direct light to get the maximum effect. The Jade Green and Mandarin Yellow are the most common translucent to opaque colors. All the other opaques are very difficult to find and command higher prices among advanced collectors.

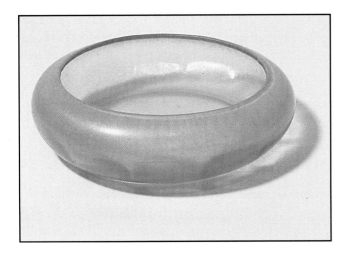

PLATE 639. Bowl, #179, shallow cupped, ground foot, Blue, 7¼"w, 1¾"h, 5½"b, $30.00

PLATE 640. Bowl, #179, shallow cupped, ground foot, Pearl Gray, 6⅞"w, 2¼"h, 5½"b, rare color, $225.00

PLATE 641. Bowl, shallow, flared rim, ground foot, Blue, 12"w, 1⅞"h, 6⅞"b, $60.00

PLATE 642. Bowl, shallow, flared rim, ground foot, light blue-green, 11⅜"w, 2¼"h, 7½"b, $60.00

PLATE 643. Bowl, shallow, flared rim, ground foot, Pearl Blue (opaque blue slag), 11"w, 2¼"h, 7½"b, rare color, $200.00

PLATE 644. Bowl, #8105, flared, Pink, 9⅜"w, 3⅜"h, 2¾"b, rare shape, $75.00

PLATE 645. Bowl, flared, 6 sets optic rays & points, translucent blue, 9¼"w, 2⅝"h, 3"b, rare color, $75.00

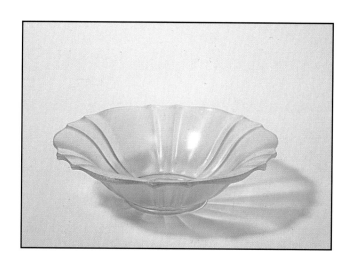

PLATE 646. Bowl, #310, flared, Green, 9⅞"w, 2¾"h, 3¾"b, $65.00

135

PLATE 647. Bowl, #314, flared, smooth rim, Crystal with green trim, 10½"w, 2⅛"h, 3⅝"b, $50.00

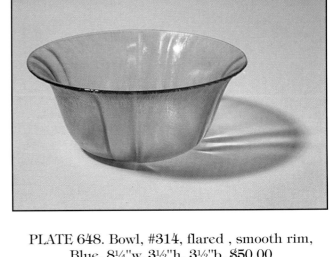

PLATE 648. Bowl, #314, flared , smooth rim, Blue, 8¼"w, 3½"h, 3½"b, $50.00

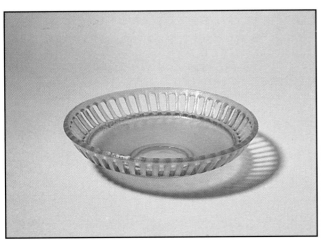

PLATE 649. Bowl, #8076, small Open Work, shallow cupped, Blue, 8⅞"w, 2¼"h, 3"b, $80.00

PLATE 650. Bowl, #8076, Open Work, flared, flat rim, Nile Green (opaque green slag), 11⅛"w, 2¼"h, 3¾"b, rare color, $400.00

PLATE 651. Bowl, #8076, Open Work, flared, flat rim, Pearl Blue (opaque blue slag), 11⅛"w, 2¼"h, 3¾"b, rare color, $300.00

PLATE 652. Bowl, #8076, Open Work, flared, rolled rim, purple slag-tortoise shell, 10½"w, 2½"h, 3¾"b, rare color, $300.00

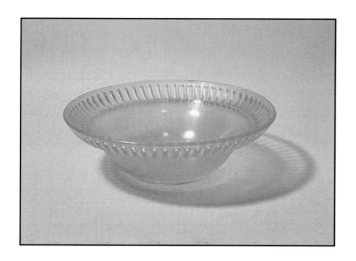

PLATE 653. Bowl, #8076, Open Work,
flared, Topaz, 10⅛"w, 3⅛"h, 3¾"b, $90.00

PLATE 654. Bowl, #8076, Open Work, flared,
cupped rim, Blue, 9"w, 3⅜"h, 4"b, $90.00

PLATE 655. Bowl, #310, 3-footed,
flared, Pink, 6"w, 2¾"h, $30.00

PLATE 656. Bowl, #310, 3-footed,
cupped, Pink, 6¼"w, 4⅛"h, $50.00

PLATE 657. Bowl, #310, 3-footed,
flared, Pink, 9¼"w, 3¼"h, $60.00

PLATE 658. Bowl, #310, 3-footed, flared, Pink
w/gold decoration, 10⅝"w, 5"h, 1½"b, $75.00

PLATE 659. Bowl, #179, flared,
Topaz, 6⅛"w, 3⅞"h, 3⅝"b, $55.00

PLATE 660. Bowl, #179, flared,
Blue, 9¼"w, 6"h, 4⅛"b, $110.00

PLATE 661. Bowl, low footed, flared, 6 sets optic
rays & points, amber, 6¼"w, 4¼"h, 3½"b, $35.00

PLATE 662. Bowl, #314, low footed, flared, light
purple, 6¾"w, 4¼"h, 3⅝"b, scarce color, $70.00

PLATE 663. Bowl, low footed, flared,
optic rays, Blue, 6¾"w, 4"h, 3½"b, $35.00

PLATE 664. Bowl, low footed, wide flared, 6 sets
optic rays & points, amber, 7"w, 3"h, 3½"b,
$45.00

PLATE 665. Bowl, low footed, wide flared
6 sets optic rays & points, Blue,
8"w, 2½"h, 3½"b, $50.00

PLATE 666. Bowl, #314, low footed,
flared raised rim, olive green,
8⅜"w, 5⅜"h, 4¾"b, unusual color, $75.00

PLATE 667. Bowl, #179, low footed, flared rim,
Blue, 9¾"w, 7¼"h, 5⅛"b, scarce size, $120.00

PLATE 668. Bowl, #314, low footed, flared rim,
Blue, 10"w, 4⅝"h, 4⅞"b, $60.00

PLATE 669. Bowl, #310, low footed, flared rim,
Blue, 10"w, 5"h, 4¼"b, $70.00

PLATE 670. Bowl, #314, low footed,
Pomona, Crystal with yellow and blue enamel,
9¾"w, 4¾"h, 5"b, $100.00

PLATE 671. Bowl, low footed, flared,
6 sets optic rays & points, Old Rose (opaque
pink), 9¾"w, 3¾"h, 4⅛"b, rare color, $325.00

PLATE 672. Bowl, #310, low footed,
Open Work, flared down rim, Topaz,
11¼"w, 6"h, 5¼"b, rare shape, $350.00

PLATE 673. Bowl, #310, low footed,
Open Work, flared flat rim, Crystal,
11½"w, 6"h, 5⅜"b, rare shape, $300.00

PLATE 674. Comport, flared, 4 sets of optic rays,
Crystal, 6⅜"w, 4¾"h, 3¼"b, scarce shape, $45.00

PLATE 675. Comport, #179, low footed,
flared, cupped, Crystal with green trim,
7⅛"w, 3⅞"h, 3⅞"b, $45.00

PLATE 676. Comport, #315, low footed,
flared, Green, 7⅜"w, 5"h, 3½"b, rare shape,
$100.00

PLATE 677. Comport, low footed, flared,
Topaz, 5⅜"w, 5"h, 3¼"b, $45.00

PLATE 678. Comport, #179, low footed,
flared, Crystal with blue and white enamel,
8⅛"w, 6½"h, 4½"b, scarce enamel, $70.00

PLATE 679. Comport, #179, low footed, flared,
Pomona, Crystal with yellow and blue enamel,
8"w, 6¾"h, 4½"b, $75.00

PLATE 680. Comport, #179, low footed, flared,
Cumula, Crystal with green and white enamel,
8"w, 6¼"h, 4½"b, $80.00

PLATE 681. Comport, low footed, wide flared,
amber, 8"w, 3⅞"h, 3⅛"b, $50.00

PLATE 682. Comport, high footed, flared,
cupped, Cumula, Crystal with green and white
enamel, 6¼"w, 4⅜"h, 3¼"b, $50.00

PLATE 683. Comport, high footed, flared, cupped, Topaz, 7½"w, 4⅝"h, 3⅝"b, $40.00

PLATE 684. Comport, #314, high footed, flared, Royal Blue (light cobalt blue), 5⅝"w, 7"h, 3¾"b, scarce color, $60.00

PLATE 685. Comport, #314, high footed, flared, light purple, 6"w, 7"h, 3¾"b, $75.00

PLATE 686. Comport, high footed, wide flared, 6 sets optic rays & points, amber, 5½"w, 6⅝"h, 3¼"b, $45.00

PLATE 687. Comport, high footed, wide flared, 6 sets optic rays & points, amber, 7¾"w, 8¼"h, 4⅜"b, $70.00

PLATE 688. Comport, #310, high footed, flared, Blue, 7⅛"w, 6⅝"h, 3¾"b, $50.00

PLATE 689. Sherbet, Mandarin Yellow (opaque yellow), 3⅝"w, 3⅜"h, 2½"b, rare shape, $50.00

PLATE 690. Sherbet, flared, 6 sets optic rays & points, Jade Green (opaque green), 4⅝"w, 2⅞"h, 3¼"b, $40.00

PLATE 691. Sherbet, Blue, 3⅞"w, 4½"h, 2⅝"b, scarce shape, $50.00

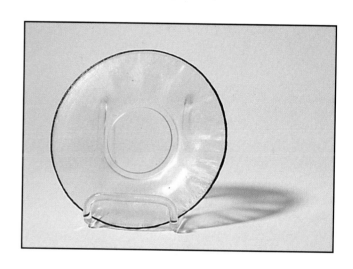

PLATE 692. Plate, 13 optic panels, Topaz with black trim, 6⅞"w, 3"b, $25.00

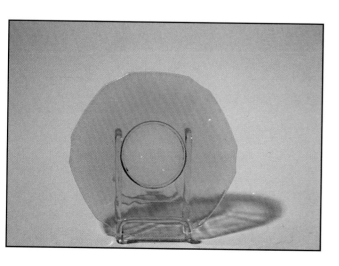

PLATE 693. Plate, 6 optic rays with points, light blue, 8"w, 3¼"b, $35.00

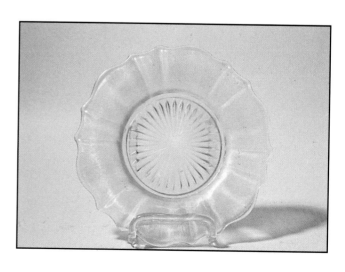

PLATE 694. Plate, #310, Pink, 8½"w, 4½"b, $40.00

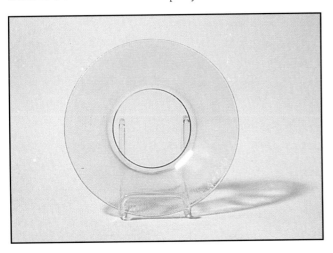

PLATE 695. Plate, 12 optic panels,
light blue, 9"w, 4¾"b, $25.00

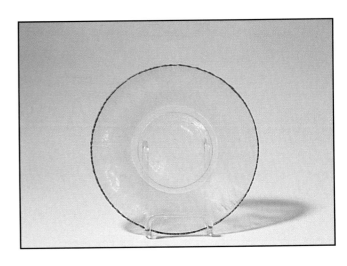

PLATE 696. Plate, 12 optic panels,
Crystal with green trim, 9⅛"w, 4¾"b, $35.00

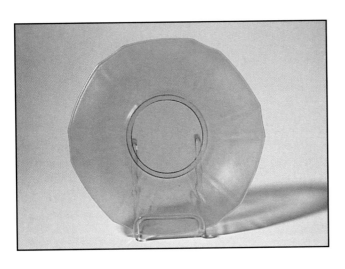

PLATE 697. Plate, 6 optic rays with points,
amber, 10¼"w, 4¼"b, scarce color, $50.00

PLATE 698. Plate, #8076, Open Work, black
amethyst, 12⅛"w, 3⅝"b, scarce color, $175.00

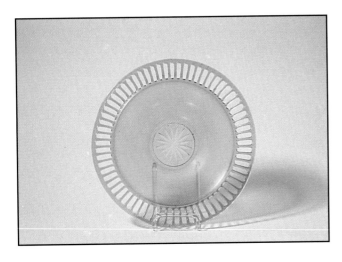

PLATE 699. Plate, #8076, Open Work,
light blue, 12½"w, 3¾"b, $125.00

PLATE 700. Plate, #8076, Open Work, Coral
(opaque yellow-orange slag), 12½"w, 3¾"b,
$300.00

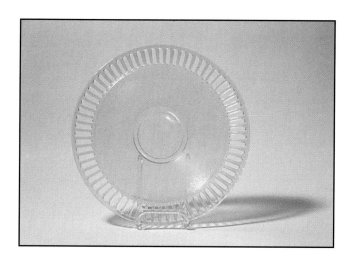

PLATE 701. Plate, #8076, Open Work,
Topaz, 12½"w, 3¾"b, $85.00

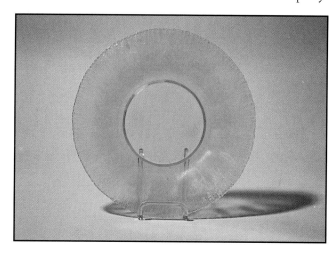

PLATE 702. Plate, 16 optic panels, Topaz,
13⅜"w, 7"b, scarce size, $90.00

PLATE 703. Plate, Bread, Topaz with black trim,
7" x 12"w, 2"h, 3¼" x 5¾"b, $50.00

PLATE 704. Plate, #310, footed cake,
Pink, 12½"w, 3⅛"h, 4¼"b, $80.00

PLATE 705. Server, handled, #179, purple,
9⅝"w, 4½"h, 3⅝"b, $120.00 ($45.00 blue)

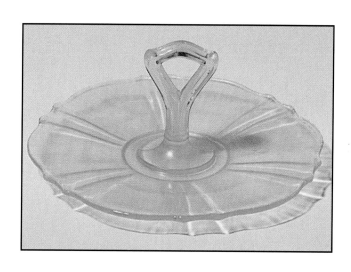

PLATE 706. Server, handled, #310,
Green, 10"w, 4"h, 3¾"b, $65.00

PLATE 707. Cheese and Cracker Set,
#320, Topaz with black trim; Cheese Dish,
4⅝"w, 2⅜"h, 3⅜"b; Plate, 9⅝"w, 5⅝"b, $60.00 set

PLATE 708. Cheese and Cracker Set, #310,
Green; Cheese Dish, 4¾"w, 3"h, 3¼"b,
Plate, 9¾"w, 5⅜"b, $80.00 set

PLATE 709. Relish Jar and Under-Plate Set,
Pink; Jar, 4½"w, 3½"h, 4¼"b;
Plate, 11¾"w, 7½"b, $125.00 set

PLATE 710. Covered Jar, Blue,
4½"w, 3½"h, 4¼"b, $80.00

PLATE 711. Candy Jar, olive green,
3½"w, 9½"h, 3⅜"b, $75.00

PLATE 712. Candy Jar, #310, Blue,
7"w, 8"h, 3¾"b, $65.00

PLATE 713. Candlesticks, #94, octagonal base, Pink, 1½"h, 3⅝"b, scarce shape, $60.00 pair

PLATE 714. Candlesticks, #151, wide base, Topaz, 7¾"h, 5"b, $100.00 pair

PLATE 715. Candlesticks, #151, wide base, Pomona, Crystal with red and green enamel, 7¾"h, 4¾"b, rare decoration, $150.00 pair

PLATE 716. Candlesticks, #151, Coral (opaque yellow-orange slag), 8¾"h, 4¼"b, $200.00 pair

PLATE 717. Candlesticks, Twist Bobèche, Topaz with black trim, 9⅜"h, 4⅜"b, $140.00 pair

PLATE 718. Candlesticks, #310, Jade Green (opaque green), 9"h, 5¼"b, $120.00 pair ($90.00 blue)

PLATE 719. Candlesticks, #315, Blue,
9½"h, 5"b, $150.00 pair

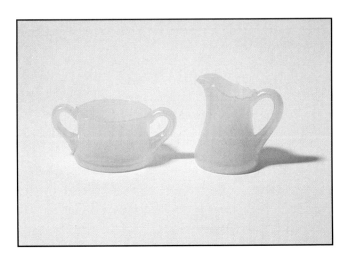

PLATE 720. Cream and Sugar Set, #310,
Mandarin Yellow (opaque yellow), scarce shape;
Creamer, 3"w, 3⅞"h, 3"b;
Sugar, 3⅜"w, 2⅜"h, 3½"b, $200.00 set

PLATE 721. Mayonnaise and Under-Plate Set,
#314, Crystal with green trim, scarce decoration;
Bowl, 6½"w, 4¼"h, 3½"b; Plate, 9¾"w, 5⅝"b,
$85.00 set

PLATE 722. Mayonnaise, Under-Plate and Ladle
Set, #310, Pink, $125.00 set; Bowl, 6"w, 2½"h,
$45.00; Plate, 8⅜"w, 4½"b, $35.00;
Ladle, 2"w, 5"h, 2"b, $45.00

PLATE 723. Mayonnaise and Under-Plate Set,
Blue; Bowl, 4¼"w, 2¼"h, 3"b; Plate, 6⅛"w, 3¼"b,
$55.00 set

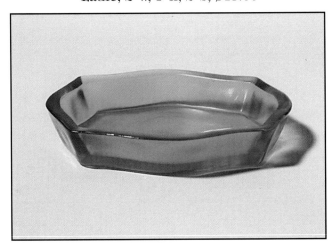

PLATE 724. Ash Tray, Blue, 3" x 4"w, ¾"h,
2⅜" x 3½"b, rare shape, $125.00

PLATE 725. Lamp Ring or Bobèche,
Blue, 4½"w, 2¼"b, $50.00

PLATE 726. Vase, #179, Sweet Pea,
Green with gold trim, 7"w, 4½"h, 3¾"b,
rare color, $75.00 ($40.00 blue)

PLATE 727. Vase, #179, hat shape,
Pomona, Crystal with red and green enamel,
9½"w, 3"h, 3⅝"b, rare decoration, $125.00

PLATE 728. Vase, #179, hat shape, opaque red
slag, 9¼"w, 2⅞"h, 3⅝"b, only one known, $500.00

PLATE 729. Vase, #179, Sweet Pea, Crystal with
black stripes, 8⅜"w, 5¾"h, 4½"b,
scarce decoration, $85.00

PLATE 730. Vase, #179, rolled rim, Pearl Blue
(opaque blue slag), 8⅝"w, 5¼"h, 4½"b, $140.00

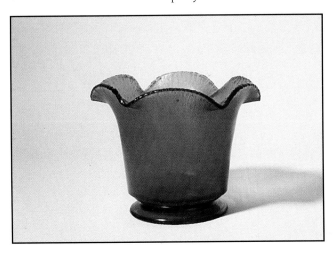

PLATE 731. Vase, #179, crimped rim,
light purple, 7½"w, 5⅞"h, 4½"b, $60.00

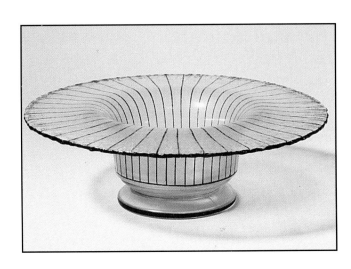

PLATE 732. Vase, #179, hat shape, Crystal with
black stripes, 11¼"w, 3⅜"h, 4½"b, $110.00

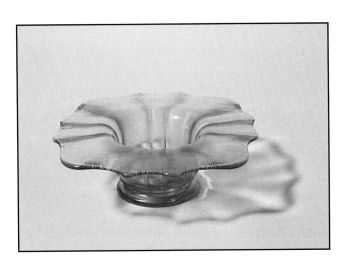

PLATE 733. Vase, #310, hat shape,
Blue, 7¾"w, 2½"h, 3"b, $90.00

PLATE 734. Vase, Old Rose (opaque pink),
3¾"w, 5¾"h, 2⅛"b, rare color, $125.00

PLATE 735. Vase, Jade Green (opaque green),
3½"w, 5⅞"h, 2⅛"b, $50.00

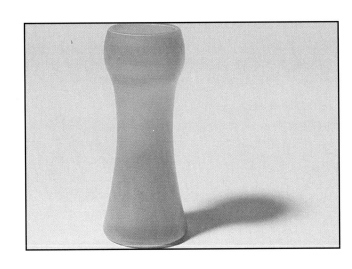

PLATE 736. Vase, Jade Green (opaque green),
2⅛"w, 6¼"h, 2⅜"b, $50.00

PLATE 737. Vase, Mandarin Yellow (opaque yellow), 4"w, 8¼"h, 3⅛"b, $75.00

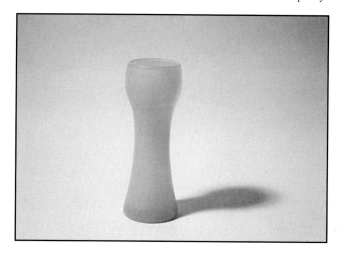

PLATE 738. Vase, Mandarin Yellow (opaque yellow), 3⅝"w, 10⅜"h, 3⅞"b, $85.00

PLATE 739. Vase, Mandarin Yellow (opaque yellow) with black trim, 6¼"w, 12"h, 4¾"b, $125.00

PLATE 740. Vase, #179, footed, flared, cupped, Topaz, 5½"w, 5⅜"h, 3⅛"b, $35.00

PLATE 741. Vase, #179, footed, flared, flattened, Blue, 6"w, 4⅝"h, 3"b, $35.00

PLATE 742. Vase, #310, Open Work, flared, cupped, Topaz, 6¾"w, 6⅞"h, 3½"b, rare shape, $150.00

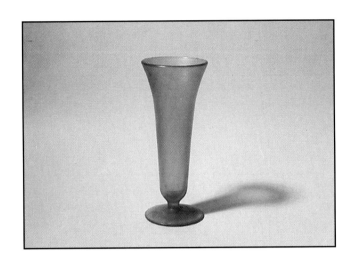

PLATE 743. Vase, #151, Blue,
3½"w, 8¼"h, 3¼"b, $50.00

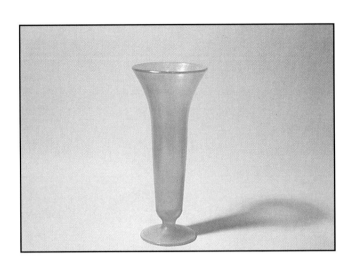

PLATE 744. Vase, #151, Topaz,
5"w, 11⅞"h, 4"b, $70.00

PLATE 745. Vase, #310, Blue,
5"w, 8¾"h, 3½"b, $80.00

PLATE 746. Vase, #151, cupped dahlia,
Green, 4⅛"w, 8⅛"h, 3½"b, $80.00

VINELAND FLINT GLASS WORKS

Vineland, New Jersey

Vineland Flint Glass Works, Vineland, New Jersey, created the Durand Art Glass Division in 1924 which resulted in the making of the famous Durand Art Glass which rivaled Tiffany, Steuben, and Fenton's freehand art glass. Though little information has been found concerning the Vineland Flint Glass Works' general tablewares, several stretch glass pieces have been found with the Vineland paper label still attached (Plate 752). From these labels, we have determined three of the actual colors and several numbers that refer to the mold and shape. Their glass quality and colors were quite variable but the following colors are known:

caramel slag – light tan with dark brown streaks, only one candlestick is known (Plate 765).

green – a green glass, similar to Florentine Green though often very light in intensity (Plate 749).

Old Gold – a yellow-orange amber glass (Plate 755).

pink – pink glass, often with a somewhat smoke colored iridescence; similar to Velva Rose of Fenton (Plate 763).

light royal blue – a light blue-purple or light cobalt glass; similar to U.S. Glass's Royal Blue (Plate 750).

cobalt blue – a dark cobalt glass with gold to silver iridescence; similar to Fenton's Royal Blue (Plate 754).

Tut Blue – a medium blue glass, similar to Celeste Blue of Fenton (Plate 751).

crystal – crystal glass with light iridescence; like Persian Pearl though the base glass often has a light green cast (Plate 748).

Wisteria – a light purple glass (Plate 753).

None of the Vineland stretch glass pieces are overly common but the wisteria, blue, amber, and crystal are the most common colors found. Any additional pieces with paper labels should be conserved as they may provide clues as to the actual color names and item numbers.

PLATE 747. Bowl, wide flared, Wisteria, (light purple), 8¾"w, 3⅛"h, 2⅞"b, $60.00

PLATE 748. Bowl, flared, crimped, crystal, 9"w, 3¼"h, 2¾"b, $45.00

PLATE 749. Bowl, flared, crimped, light blue-green, 9¼"w, 3"h, 2⅞"b, rare color, $75.00

PLATE 750. Bowl, flared, crimped, light cobalt blue, 8½"w, 3¼"h, 2¾"b, rare color, $75.00

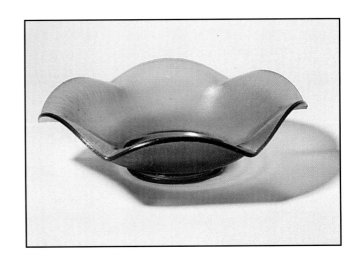

PLATE 751. Bowl, #12, flared, crimped, Tut Blue (blue), 10⅝"w, 3"h, 3⅞"b, $75.00

PLATE 752. Bowl with label, see Plate 751

PLATE 753. Bowl, flared, crimped, Wisteria, (light purple), 11¼"w, 4½"h, 4⅜"b, $90.00

PLATE 754. Bowl, flared, cobalt blue, 7½"w, 4"h, 4⅜"b, rare color, $150.00

PLATE 755. Bowl, cupped, Old Gold (amber), 6¾"w, 3⅞"h, 4⅜"b, $60.00

PLATE 756. Bowl, rolled rim, Wisteria (purple),
7⅝"w, 3⅛"h, 4⅜"b, $65.00

PLATE 757. Bowl, flared, crimped,
Wisteria (purple), 8¼"w, 3¾"h, 4⅜"b, $70.00

PLATE 758. Candlesticks, (Central Glass not
Vineland, for comparison with Plate 759),
7¼"h, 3⅞"b, $75.00 pair

PLATE 759. Candlesticks, light pink-purple,
7"h, 4"b, rare color, $90.00 pair

PLATE 760. Candlesticks, thick base,
Wisteria (dark purple), 6¾"h, 4"b, $80.00 pair

PLATE 761. Candlesticks, thick base,
Wisteria (light purple), 6¾"h, 4"b, scarce color,
$95.00 pair

PLATE 762. Candlesticks, light blue/green, 8"h, 4¼"b, rare shape, $90.00 pair

PLATE 763. Candlesticks, pink, 9⅞"h, 4¼"b, scarce color, $140.00 pair ($110.00 blue)

PLATE 764. Candlesticks, Old Gold (amber), 10"h, 4¼"b, scarce color, $170.00 pair

PLATE 765. Candlesticks, opaque caramel slag, 10⅛"h, 4¼"b, only one known, $400.00 pair

PLATE 766. Vase, Wisteria (dark purple), 2⅛"w, 7"h, 2⅝"b, scarce shape, $85.00

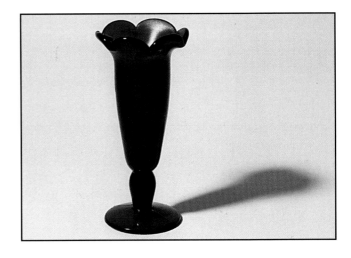

PLATE 767. Vase, cobalt blue, 3"w, 6½"h, 2⅝"b, scarce shape/color, $95.00

Unattributed and Confusing Pieces

Unattributed Pieces

In spite of the best research and comparing of glass colors, forms, and iridescence, there are several pieces of stretch glass that cannot be currently attributed to a manufacturer. Though we may have a feel of who made some of these pieces, we have opted to list them as simply unattributed or unidentified.

If any documentation, such as an advertisement, label or unique color, is found associated with any of these pieces, we would greatly appreciate hearing about it.

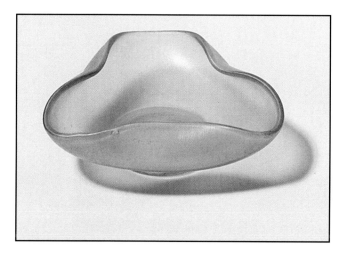

PLATE 768. Bowl, three cupped, green,
7¼"w, 2¼"h, 3¼"b, $35.00

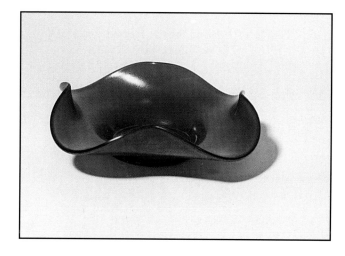

PLATE 769. Bowl, flared, four cupped,
cobalt blue, 8⅞"w, 2¼"h, 3¼"b, scarce color,
$65.00

PLATE 770. Bowl, wide flared, crystal,
10¼"w, 7⅞"h, 3⅞"b, only one known, $100.00

PLATE 771. Bowl, rolled rim, amber,
9⅞"w, 2½"h, 4"b, $70.00

PLATE 772. Bowl, three footed, crystal,
7¾"w, 3¼"h, $50.00

PLATE 773. Comport, olive green,
6⅝"w, 5"h, 3⅜"b, $90.00

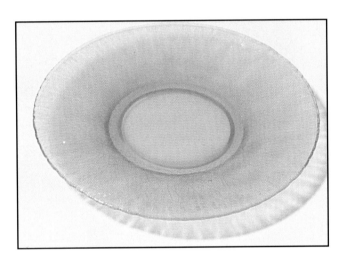

PLATE 774. Plate, ground foot, light olive green,
7¾"w, 3¾"b, rare color, $50.00

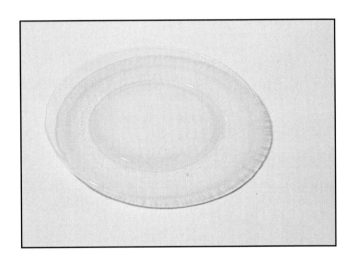

PLATE 775. Plate, ground foot,
crystal opalescent, 8½"w, 5"b, rare color, $65.00

PLATE 776. Plate, crystal with black design
9¾"w, 2⅝"b, $250.00

PLATE 777. Server, handled, 24 panels, crystal
with blue enamel, 10½"w, 4¼"h, 4"b, $45.00

PLATE 778. Jar, biscuit with metal trim and lid,
rib optic, blue, 5¼"w, 7¾"h, 3⅞"b,
only one known, $350.00

PLATE 779. Basket, 8-sided, green,
4½"w, 2¼"h, 3¾"b, only one known, $125.00

PLATE 780. Pitcher, pontil base,
blue, 3¾"w, 8⅞"h, 5"b, $150.00

PLATE 781. Pitcher and Tumbler, marigold
with black feet, wheel cut decoration;
Pitcher, 4⅜"w, 8⅜"h, 2¾"b, $450.00;
Tumbler, 3"w, 4⅞"h, 3"b, $100.00 each

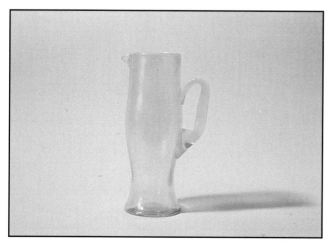

PLATE 782. Pitcher, crystal with topaz handle,
3½"w, 10½"h, 3¾"b, $250.00

PLATE 783. Pitcher, blue with topaz handle,
4¼"w, 10½"h, 3¾"b, $250.00

159

PLATE 784. Pitcher and Tumbler, green, $300.00 set; Pitcher, pontil base, 3¾"w, 10¼"h, 3¾"b, $150.00; Tumbler, 3"w, 5"h, 2¼"b, $25.00 each

PLATE 785. Pitcher and Tumbler, marigold with crystal handle, $335.00 set; Pitcher, pontil base, 5"w, 6⅛"h, 3¾"b, $125.00; Tumbler, 2⅞"w, 4"h, 2¼"b, $35.00 each

PLATE 786. Lamp, kerosene, purple, 3⅛"w, 8"h, 2⅝"b, only one known, $300.00

PLATE 787. Lamp shade, electric, flared, crimped, dark green, 6"w, 3⅝"h, 2¼"b, rare shape/color, $90.00

PLATE 788. Lamp shade, electric, green with marigold, 8"w, 2⅝"h, 2¼"b, scarce color, $70.00

PLATE 789. Lamp shade, electric, cupped, milk glass with pearl iridescence, 4¾"w, 4½"h, 2¼"b, $55.00

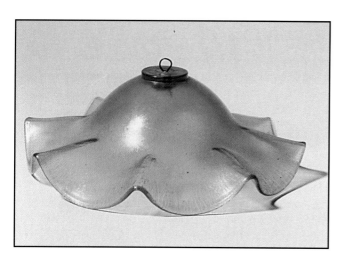

PLATE 790. Smoke shade, crimped, olive green, 7⅞"w, 2½"h, 1¼"b, rare shape/color, $150.00

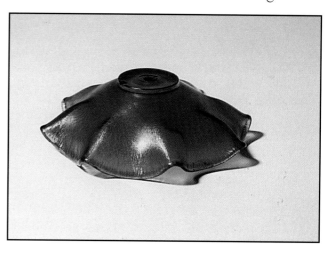

PLATE 791. Shade or tray base, hole in center, purple, 5¾"w, 1¾"h, 1½"b, $65.00

PLATE 792. Vase, crimped top, green, 8"w, 6"h, 3¼"b, $65.00

PLATE 793. Vase, green, 3¼"w, 6¾"h, 2¼"b, only two known, $90.00

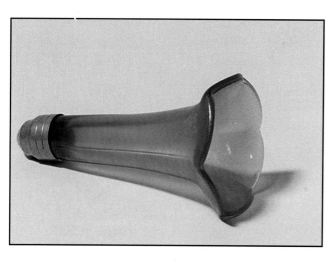

PLATE 794. Vase, car, crimped, blue with metal base, 3⅛"w, 6⅛"h, 1"b, $75.00

PLATE 795. Cologne, blue, 1⅛"w, 5¾"h, 1⅜"b, $150.00

Carnival Glass with Stretch Effect

Iridescent glass, that today we call carnival, was introduced to the American consumers between 1900 and 1905. During the manufacturing process, any pieces with crizzled or stretch effects were considered defective and were generally destroyed. However, there are always a few examples that escaped being culled.

On the other hand, later in the carnival glass production period, there seem to have been deliberate attempts by several manufacturers to create more interest in their iridescent glass by producing stretch effects in pieces that normally had plain iridescence.

True American stretch glass was made to imitate the more expensive art glass of the period. Tiffany, Stuben, Cartier, and European makers were producing desirable, iridescent ornamental pieces that cost considerably more than the average home owner could afford. American manufacturers of press mold products had been making iridescent wares, which we call carnival glass today. They knew that reheating this carnival glass resulted in a stretch effect. When this effect was created on plain glassware, it resembled the more expensive art glasses. Soon these companies were in full production of this "poor man's art glass."

For those who own and appreciate escapes or transition pieces, they are fortunate to have the interesting patterns associated with true carnival glass as well as the elegant iridescent effects associated with stretch glass.

PLATE 796. Bowl, flared, cupped, Fenton #1091, Open Work Basket Weave, Celeste Blue, 5"w, 1¾"h, 1⅜"b, $300.00

PLATE 797. Bowl, flared, crimped top, Fenton #1093, Open Work Basket Weave, Florentine Green, 8¼"w, 3½"h, 2⅞"b, $750.00

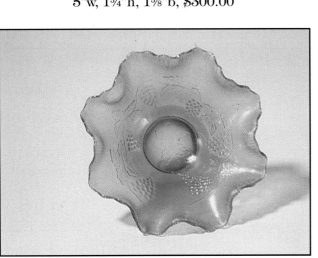

PLATE 798. Bowl, crimped top, Diamond Vintage, blue, 8¼"w, 3⅞"h, 3⅞"b, $850.00

PLATE 799. Bowl, crimped edge, Fenton Plaid, Celeste Blue, 9⅛"w, 2½"h, 3¼"b, $4,000.00

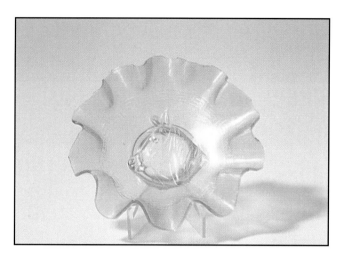

PLATE 800. Bowl, crimped and clipped edge,
Diamond Pony, blue, 8⅝"w, 2⅝"h, 3⅛"b,
$1,000.00

PLATE 801. Bowl, candy-ribbon edge,
Fenton Vintage, Celeste Blue, 10"w, 2⅝"h, 3⅞"b,
only one known, $4,500.00

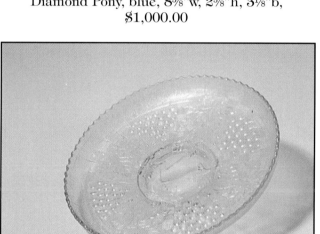

PLATE 802. Bowl, wide flared, Northwood Grape
and Cable, crystal, 11⅛"w, 1⅞"h, 4¼"b, $300.00

PLATE 803. Bowl, footed, crimped, Diamond
Double Stem Rose, blue, 8½"w, 4"h, 4"b,
$150.00

PLATE 804. Nappy, handled, Diamond
Windflower, green, 6¼"w, 3½"h, 3⅜"b,
six known, $500.00

PLATE 805. Bonbon, two-handled, Fenton Persian Medallion, Celeste Blue, 7½"w, 2½"h, 2¾"b,
three known, $1,200.00

PLATE 806. Comport, raised rim,
Fenton Stippled Rays, Wisteria (light purple),
4⅞"w, 4⅜"h, 3⅛"b, $125.00

PLATE 807. Comport, wide raised rim,
Fenton Stippled Rays, Topaz,
6¼"w, 3½"h, 3⅛"b, $120.00

PLATE 808. Comport, crimped, Fenton Stippled
Rays, Celeste Blue, 7"w, 3½"h, 3⅛"b, $275.00

PLATE 809. Comport, crimped, Diamond Coin
Spot, green, 6¼"w, 4¼"h, 3⅜"b, $225.00

PLATE 810. Plate, Northwood Grape and
Cable, purple, 9⅛"w, 3½"b, $250.00

PLATE 811. Plate, Imperial Heavy Grape,
crystal with blue smoke iridescence,
11⅛"w, 5¼"b, $1,000.00

PLATE 812. Plate, Imperial Homestead,
crystal with blue smoke iridescence,
10⅝"w, 4¼"b, $1,000.00

PLATE 813. Plate, Imperial Homestead,
marked NUART, amber, 10⅝"w, 4¼"b, $1,200.00

PLATE 814. Basket, handled, Imperial Plain
Jane, green, 2¾" x 4½"w, 7⅝"h, 2¾"b, $125.00

PLATE 815. Vase, Northwood Tornado,
dark purple, 5½"w, 6½"h, 3"b, $2,750.00

PLATE 816. Vase, Diamond Pulled Loops,
blue, 3⅞"w, 11¼"h, 3⅜"b, $750.00

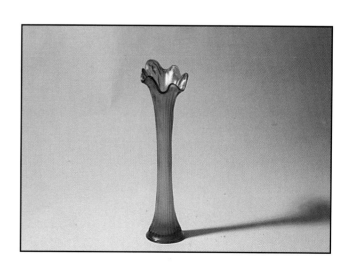

PLATE 817. Vase, Northwood Fine Rib, blue,
4¾"w, 16"h, 3¾"b, $650.00

New Stretch Glass

The spraying of metallic salt solutions on hot glass has been performed many times since the discovery of carnival glass and stretch glass. Several American companies have made iridescent glass, occasionally with stretch effect, since the mid-1930s, the time we consider that the "original" stretch glass manufacturing ceased.

The Fenton Art Glass Company has been the most prolific producer of modern stretch glass, and we compliment their efforts to mark all these recent pieces. These recent pieces have acquired a following of collectors and even collectors of old stretch glass often enjoy collecting the newer pieces.

PLATE 818. Bowl, rolled rim, Fenton #2747RX, ca. 1993, red with gold leaf decoration, 10¼"w, 1⅝"h, 5¾"b, $110.00

PLATE 819. Comport, Fenton Persian Medallion, ca. 1983, Velva Blue, 5¾"w, 6½"h, 3⅛"b, $35.00

PLATE 820. Pitcher and Tumbler set, Fenton/ Levay, ca. 1976, 7-piece, dark purple, $250.00 set; Pitcher, crimped rim 5¼"w, 10¼"h, 4"b, $150.00; Tumbler, 2½"w, 4"h, 2½"b, $20.00 each

PLATE 821. Pitcher and Glass, Stiegel Green, ca. 1994; Pitcher, 8-sided, 4¾"w, 7⅞"h, 3½"b, $70.00; Glass, stemmed, 6-panels 3¼"w, 6"h, 3¼"b, $20.00 each

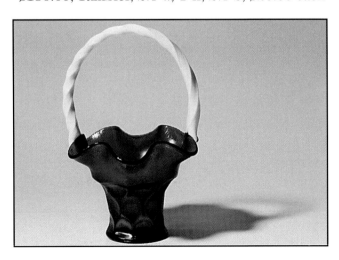

PLATE 822. Basket, from Fenton Georgian tumbler, ca. 1993, purple with milk glass handle, 6¼"w, 9"h, 2¾"b, $75.00

PLATE 823. Basket, from Fenton Georgian
tumbler, ca. 1993, purple with purple handle,
6"w, 8¼"h, 2¾"b, $50.00

PLATE 824. Basket, from Fenton #847
Melon-Rib, ca. 1993, purple with purple handle,
8"w, 7¾"h, 3⅜"b, $60.00

PLATE 825. Epergne, Fenton experimental,
only one in Fenton Museum, ruby,
11½"w, 12¾"h, 5½"b, $650.00

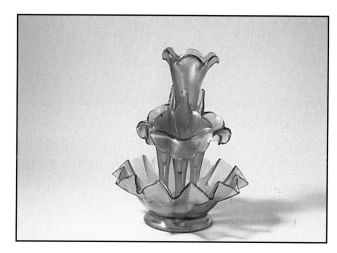

PLATE 826. Epergne, Fenton, ca. 1995,
Stiegel Green, 11"w, 13½"h, 5½"b, $250.00

PLATE 827. Bell, Fenton, green,
3½"w, 6"h, $40.00

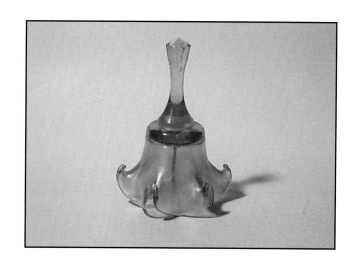

PLATE 828. Bell, crimped rim,
Fenton 75th Anniversary, ca. 1982,
Velva Rose, 4½"w, 6¾"h, $40.00

PLATE 829. Vase, spittoon shape, Fenton 75th Anniversary, ca. 1982, Velva Rose, 6¼"w, 4¾"h, 3⅜"b, $65.00

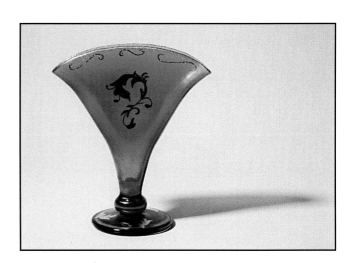

PLATE 830. Vase, fan, Fenton, ca. 1993, Twilight Blue with gold decoration, 1⅝" x 7½"w, 8½"h, 3⅞"b, $90.00

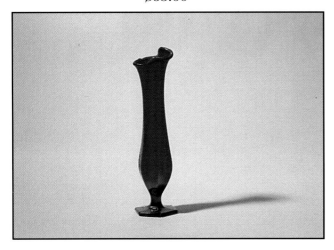

PLATE 831. Vase, 6-sided, Fenton, red, 3"w, 12⅜"h, 3"b, $100.00

PLATE 832. Vase, fan, Fenton Twin-Dolphin, Ocean Blue with decoration, 1½" x 6⅜"w, 5¾"h, 3½"b, $65.00

PLATE 833. Vase, fan, Fenton Twin-Dolphin, 20th Anniversary Stretch Glass Society, 1994, red, 1½" x 6"w, 6"h, 3½"b, $90.00

PLATE 834. Vase, square, Fenton Twin-Dolphin, Stretch Glass Society, 1996, light cobalt, 6¼"w, 5¼"h, 3½"b, $50.00

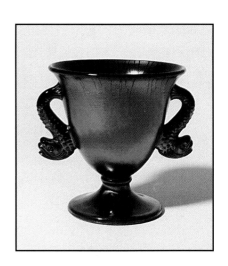

PLATE 835. Vase, round, Fenton Twin-Dolphin, Stretch Glass Society, 1997, opaque black, 4¾"w, 5⅜"h, 3½"b, $70.00

Often Mistaken Look-Alikes

Of most concern to collectors of true stretch glass has been the introduction of unmarked European pieces. Most of these were introduced in the 1960s, but there is evidence that similar pieces are still being imported. All of these pieces have excellent iridescence and a smoothed pontil mark. This true pontil is not like the ground maries found on pieces of Northwood, Fenton, and Diamond. If you run your fingernail across the edge of old ground maries, it will encounter a distinct ridge. The new pieces have smooth rims with no ridge.

Our records indicate that most of these European pieces were imported at costs of $3.75 to $10.00 each, wholesale. One importer was Koscherak Brothers, Inc. that had showrooms operated by distributors in New York, Chicago, Los Angeles, and Dallas during the early 1970s. Their 1970 advertising sheet lists seven vases (4" to 10" high), four hat vases (4" to 8" diameter), three plates (6" to 11" diameter), a 6" diameter bowl, and 3" tall tumbler.

Koscherak advertised ruby, blue (a cobalt blue), amber, and green (a dark green). Other pieces have been seen in black amethyst and crystal.

A number of these pieces have the name Posinger scratched in script onto the bottom and some others have paper labels that state Made in West Germany and Crown Glass Works. Unfortunately, we have seen these European imports marked old stretch glass or art glass and priced at $100.00 to $300.00 or even more!

Some even have LCT scratched into the pontil and others have a crude Steuben mark etched on the bottom. These pieces are obviously marked to fool unaware customers. Use caution when considering such marked pieces unless you are experienced with true Steuben and Tiffany pieces.

PLATE 836. Plate, ground pontil, cobalt blue, West Germany, 7"w, 1¾"h, 2½"b, $60.00

PLATE 837. Vase, crimped top, black opaque, West Germany, 5½"w, 3⅝"h, 2¼"b, $80.00

PLATE 838. Vase, dark green, West Germany, 5½"w, 4¼"h, 2½"b, $65.00

PLATE 839. Vase, red, West Germany, 3⅞"w, 10"h, 3⅜"b, $150.00

Identification of Similar Stretch Glass Pieces

Competition among the glass manufacturers was very strong at the turn of the century. Some companies seemed to specialize in what was known as common tableware while others specialized in ornamental glassware. Most of the major manufacturers of stretch glass manufactured both types of glass, and they were constantly aware of any new items that competing manufacturers brought to the market. If anyone seemed to develop an item that sold well, the other companies soon made similar, almost identical pieces. These similar pieces are often difficult to differentiate, especially without considerable study and inspection.

In this chapter, we will compare some of the more commonly misidentified, look-alike pieces. In some cases, careful measurements may be needed to separate the manufacturers. We will often refer to mold marks which are the seam lines left in the glass where the mold sections were joined. Experts at identification of glass carefully inspect all the edge surfaces of a piece of molded glass. The points where the mold parts joined, especially along the foot (or marie), often give clues about the type of mold used and the manufacturer.

Many pieces have been identified because of some unique color. In general, Fenton made Tangerine and Northwood made Jade Blue, Ivory, and Russet stretch glass exclusively. Therefore, when a piece is found in one of these colors, more certain identification can be made.

Stretch glass plates are probably the most difficult to identify and we make little attempt to identify most plates that contain no characteristic bases, optic panels, rays or other patterns. Considerable research remains to be done to measure and identify these items.

Many manufacturers made similar candlesticks, covered bonbons, candy jars, handled trays, cheese and cracker sets, ground marie plates, and 8" – 10" diameter fruit or flower bowls. In this chapter we will try to indicate helpful marks or other characteristics we use to identify these pieces.

Candlesticks

Many of the glass companies made similar candlesticks. The ones commonly called "Colonial," "trumpet," and "spindle" are the most confusing.

"Colonial" candlesticks were made by many companies, but Fenton, Northwood, and Vineland are the only companies known that iridized them and placed this form in their stretch lines. Fenton and Northwood made theirs in a two-piece mold (two seams) while Vineland used a three-piece mold (three seams). Northwood candlesticks have a characteristic ball finial at the top of the base while Fenton and Vineland used a more gentle slope.

"Trumpet" candlesticks are round with small narrow necks and flared bases. They were usually made in 6" (small) (Central, Northwood, and Vineland) and 8" (tall) (Central and Diamond) versions. The small trumpets are fairly easy to identify if you look at the candlestick cup height and shape and the number of rings just below the cup holder. The tall trumpets are much more difficult to identify unless you have the two types side by side. The Diamond tall trumpets have a flat slope along the base and they are commonly decorated with a white enamel ring at the base and top. The Central tall trumpets are smoothly rounded at the base and have not been seen with the enamel ring decoration. Small differences also are seen in the cup holder rings.

"Spindle" candlesticks are also difficult to separate when they are seen alone. However, when they are placed side-by-side, they are distinctly different. The Diamond and Imperial candlesticks have the middle spindle with the wide section low while the Vineland candlestick has the wide section high. The Diamond and Vineland candlesticks have rounded, narrow upper and lower rings, while the Imperial Premium has thin, sharper-edged narrow rings.

Covered Bonbons

Nearly identical covered bonbons were made by Fenton, Northwood, and Diamond. Separated lids or bottoms are especially difficult to identify. When looking at the lids, the obvious difference is the presence of a lid "lip". Northwood and Diamond lids have indented lips while Fenton lids are straight sided. The Fenton knob collar is thick and straight sided while the Diamond collar is thin and rounded.

The obvious difference in bottoms occurs in the Diamond piece. Where the panels meet the upper collar, the Diamond pieces have a straight line. The Fenton and Northwood panels are rounded at their edges. The Fenton bottom has a narrow stem and a distinct mold seam that crosses the upper collar. The Northwood bottom has a thicker stem and no mold seam that crosses the upper collar.

Colonial Style Candy Jars

These candy jars have six panels separated by flat ribs. Both Fenton and Northwood made one-pound and half-pound versions.

The Fenton lids have straight-sided lip rims while the Northwood lids are indented. The bases of the one-pound jars are very difficult to differentiate. The Fenton version has a thinner foot with the mold seam following the left side of the ribs (when looking straight at the jar). The Northwood jar has a thicker foot and the mold seam follows the right side of the ribs.

The half-pound bottoms have the same mold seams but the bowl of the Fenton version is more rounded where the foot is attached.

A similar jar made by Diamond has the panels but no rays. There is also a set of rings located at the top of the Diamond panels (Plate 60).

Handled Trays

Most of the glass companies made a handled sandwich or fruit tray. Almost all can be easily identified by carefully inspecting the shape of the handle and the point where the handle is joined to the tray.

Heart handled trays were made by Imperial and Diamond. The Diamond tray has a small heart form and the Imperial tray has a large heart-shaped loop. The Imperial trays are also eight-sided.

Loop handled trays were made by Fenton and U.S. Glass. Loop handles are rounded at the top and sides. The U.S. Glass trays are more triangular in shape while the Fenton tray is a broad loop. The U.S. Glass #310 tray has the characteristic set of six paired rays in the tray.

Shovel handled trays are the most difficult to identify; this form was made by Diamond, Imperial, Jeannette, Lancaster, and Northwood. These trays are characterized by a handle with a straight top, and often, straight sides. The Lancaster and Northwood forms are nearly triangular in outline with the Northwood handle being thin and the Lancaster one being thick. The Lancaster handle also has a ring where the handle joins the tray. Of the remaining straight-sided forms, the narrow-handled Jeannette form is the most distinctive. The Imperial shovel handled form has the handle panels continuing into the base ring where it attaches to the tray. The Diamond and Jeannette versions have the handle panels ending at a distinct ring above the tray ring. The Diamond handle tray ring is 3" in diameter while the Jeannette one is 2" in diameter.

Candlesticks

"Colonial"

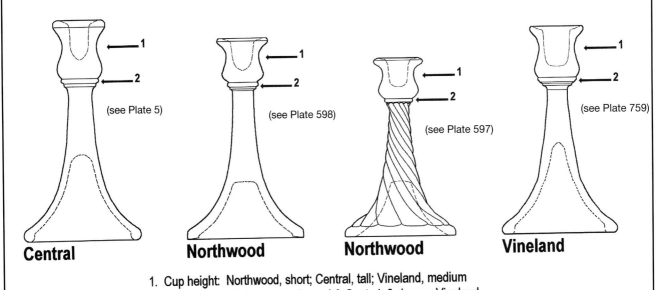

(see Plate 243)

(see Plate 601)

(see Plate 763)

Fenton

Northwood

Vineland

1. Mold seams: 2 seams = Fenton, Northwood; 3 seams = Vineland
2. Stem finial: ball = Northwood; sloped = Fenton, Vineland

Short "Trumpet"

(see Plate 5)

(see Plate 598)

(see Plate 597)

(see Plate 759)

Central

Northwood

Northwood

Vineland

1. Cup height: Northwood, short; Central, tall; Vineland, medium
2. Holder rings: 2 rings = Northwood & Central; 3 rings = Vineland

Candlesticks
Tall "Trumpet"

1. Cup Rim: Central, rounded & no mold seam;
   Diamond, angular & mold seam
2. Second holder ring: Central, straight sholder & cove in;
   Diamond, rounded out
3. Base: Central, rounded & no seam;
   Diamond, straight sided & mold seam

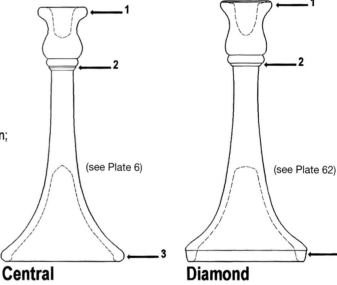

(see Plate 6)

(see Plate 62)

Central   **Diamond**

"Spindle"

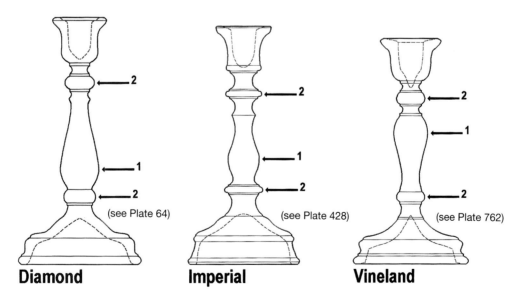

(see Plate 64)

(see Plate 428)

(see Plate 762)

Diamond   **Imperial**   **Vineland**

1. Middle spindle wide section: Diamond & Imperial, at bottom; Vineland, at top
2. Top & bottom rings: Diamond's & Vineland's are thick; Imperial's are thin

Covered Bonbons

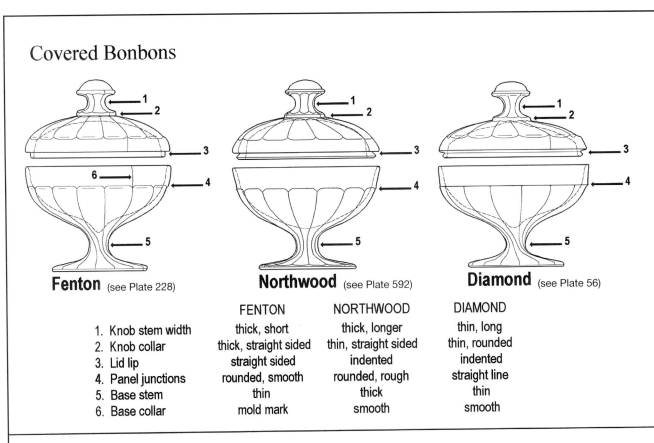

Fenton (see Plate 228)   **Northwood** (see Plate 592)   **Diamond** (see Plate 56)

	FENTON	NORTHWOOD	DIAMOND
1. Knob stem width	thick, short	thick, longer	thin, long
2. Knob collar	thick, straight sided	thin, straight sided	thin, rounded
3. Lid lip	straight sided	indented	indented
4. Panel junctions	rounded, smooth	rounded, rough	straight line
5. Base stem	thin	thick	thin
6. Base collar	mold mark	smooth	smooth

Candy Jars
One Pound   Half Pound

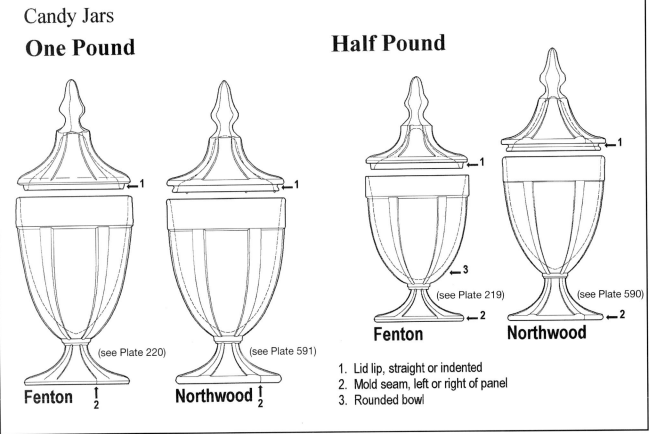

Fenton (see Plate 220)   Northwood (see Plate 591)   Fenton (see Plate 219)   Northwood (see Plate 590)

1. Lid lip, straight or indented
2. Mold seam, left or right of panel
3. Rounded bowl

Cheese and Cracker Sets

Cheese dishes can be separated by the size, shape, and number of rings on the stem. The Lancaster dish has no rings while the Northwood dish has only one ring directly under the dish. The Diamond, Fenton, and Imperial dishes have a ring under the dish and another one where the stem meets the foot. The Fenton rings are straight sided and the lower ring is very thin. The Diamond dish has the upper ring slanted at a near 45-degree angle while the stem ring is straight sided. The Imperial dish ring is straight sided while the stem ring is cut in at a distinct angle. The dish margins are also relatively distinctive as illustrated in the line drawings.

The under-plates are also difficult to identify without careful observation and exact measurements. The Fenton plate has a molded foot while the others have ground bases. The Imperial plate has the dish ring formed as a depression, not a distinct ring of glass. The Diamond, Lancaster, and Northwood plates have ground bases and distinct rings. The inside diameter of the Diamond ring is 3⅜", the Lancaster ring is 3", and the Northwood ring is 3½". The inside diameters of the ground foot are Diamond, 5"; Lancaster, 5⅛"; and Northwood, 5⅛".

Ground Marie Plates

Three companies made 8" plates with ground maries — Diamond, Fenton, and Northwood. The marie is a small foot or knob by which the piece can be picked up for shaping and applying iridescent dope. This marie is then ground off in the finishing room. This ground marie is often confused with a true pontil.

A pontil is the mark left where a rod containing a hot glob of glass is temporarily attached to a piece of glass, usually true art glass. Once the glass piece is finished, the rod is struck and the attachment point snaps loose. This pontil may be left rough or ground to a smooth circle.

To identify ground marie stretch glass plates, look for the presence or absence of a mold seam on the bottom rim (or foot). This mold seam will be a distinct ridge that will catch a finger nail scraped along the surface. The Northwood #630 plate has no mold seam. The Diamond and Fenton #630 plates have mold seams, but the Fenton plate has a distinct flat ring surface adjacent to the mold seam.

8" – 10" Fruit or Flower Bowls

Bowls made by Diamond and Lancaster look very much alike and have been dubbed 45-degree or straight-side bowls because the sides are very straight and almost at a 45-degree angle. The Lancaster bowl has a rounded shoulder and the basal foot is rounded with a small internal ring visible. Lancaster bowls are usually enameled and/or decorated with flower designs. The Diamond bowls have a distinct, thin shoulder that is straight sided. The basal foot is thick and almost flat where it sits.

The rest of the bowls may be flared, cupped, rolled over, or crimped, but the shoulder and base characteristics will remain consistent in size and form. The Fenton #600 and Vineland 10" bowls have a thick, straight-sided shoulder. The Vineland bowl has a deeper depression inside the base and a 3¾" diameter base. The Fenton bowl is slightly larger at 3⅞" diameter.

The Central bowl has a very thin shoulder ring and the bowl is generally thin and light-weight when held.

The Diamond and Northwood bowls have rounded shoulders without defined seams. The Diamond bowl is thick, feels heavy, and the upper rim has a distinct seam. The Northwood #647 bowl has a shallow foot while the #660 has a deep depression within the foot.

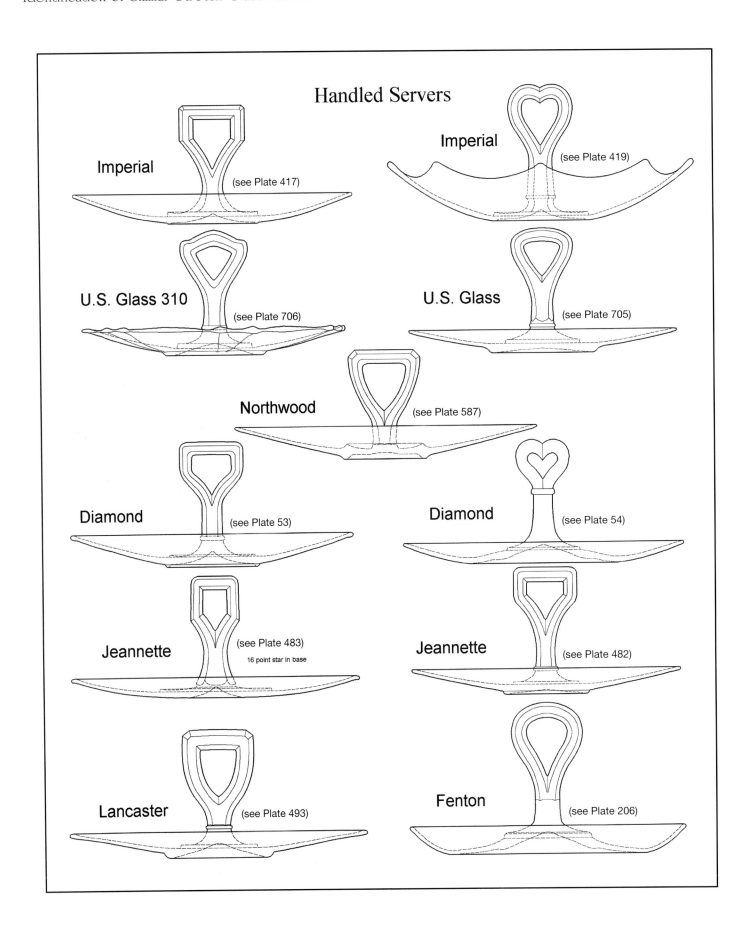

Handled Servers

Imperial (see Plate 417)

Imperial (see Plate 419)

U.S. Glass 310 (see Plate 706)

U.S. Glass (see Plate 705)

Northwood (see Plate 587)

Diamond (see Plate 53)

Diamond (see Plate 54)

Jeannette (see Plate 483)
16 point star in base

Jeannette (see Plate 482)

Lancaster (see Plate 493)

Fenton (see Plate 206)

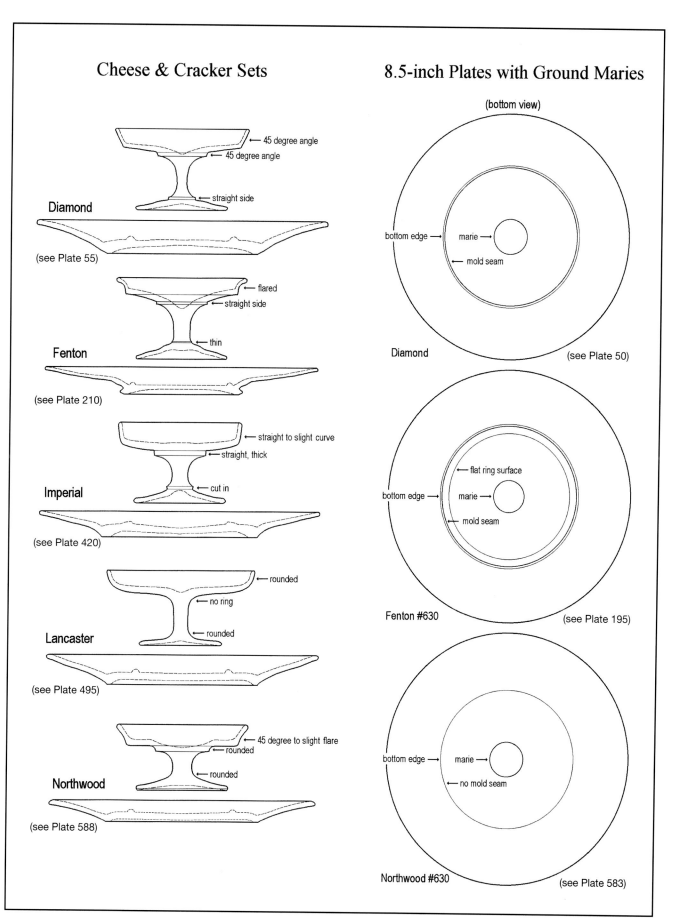

Cheese & Cracker Sets

Diamond — 45 degree angle / 45 degree angle / straight side
(see Plate 55)

Fenton — flared / straight side / thin
(see Plate 210)

Imperial — straight to slight curve / straight, thick / cut in
(see Plate 420)

Lancaster — rounded / no ring / rounded
(see Plate 495)

Northwood — 45 degree to slight flare / rounded / rounded
(see Plate 588)

8.5-inch Plates with Ground Maries

(bottom view)

Diamond — bottom edge / marie / mold seam
(see Plate 50)

Fenton #630 — bottom edge / flat ring surface / marie / mold seam
(see Plate 195)

Northwood #630 — bottom edge / marie / no mold seam
(see Plate 583)

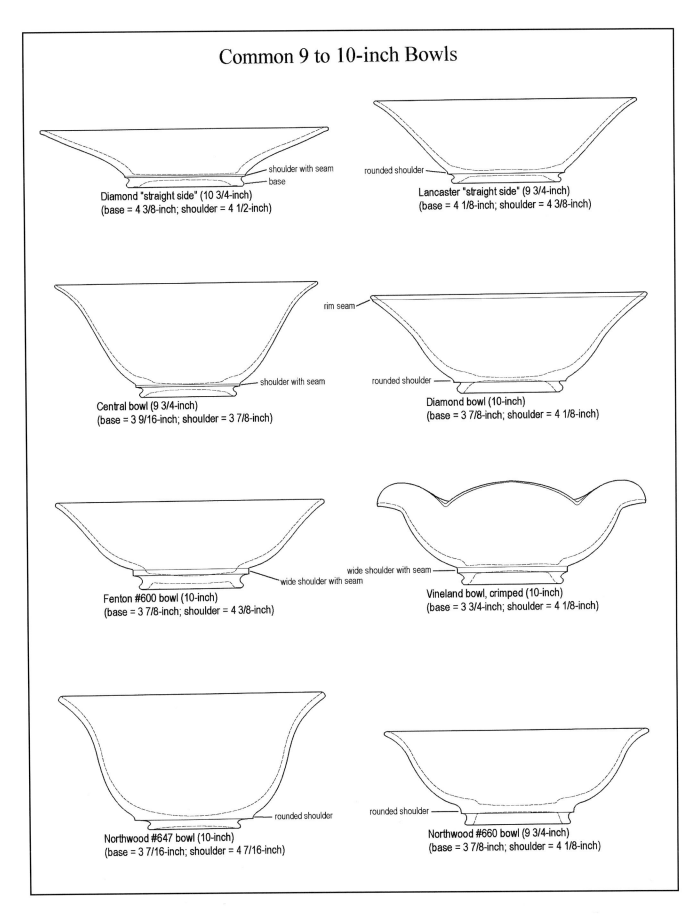

Common 9 to 10-inch Bowls

shoulder with seam
base
Diamond "straight side" (10 3/4-inch)
(base = 4 3/8-inch; shoulder = 4 1/2-inch)

rounded shoulder
Lancaster "straight side" (9 3/4-inch)
(base = 4 1/8-inch; shoulder = 4 3/8-inch)

shoulder with seam
Central bowl (9 3/4-inch)
(base = 3 9/16-inch; shoulder = 3 7/8-inch)

rim seam
rounded shoulder
Diamond bowl (10-inch)
(base = 3 7/8-inch; shoulder = 4 1/8-inch)

wide shoulder with seam
Fenton #600 bowl (10-inch)
(base = 3 7/8-inch; shoulder = 4 3/8-inch)

wide shoulder with seam
Vineland bowl, crimped (10-inch)
(base = 3 3/4-inch; shoulder = 4 1/8-inch)

rounded shoulder
Northwood #647 bowl (10-inch)
(base = 3 7/16-inch; shoulder = 4 7/16-inch)

rounded shoulder
Northwood #660 bowl (9 3/4-inch)
(base = 3 7/8-inch; shoulder = 4 1/8-inch)

Appendix

Previous Books: Authors' Perspectives

As authors, we feel quite anxious about commenting on the glass books of fellow authors. However, many early books were written without the ever emerging information that comes from diligent research. Modern archeologists and individuals interested in glass history occasionally make a "find" when an original advertising booklet is discovered. Others are sifting through the piles and piles of business papers that still exist from various old glass companies. Occasionally one of these papers yields some insight as to colors and forms made by a particular company. Still others try to gain access to old cullet piles and dumps where old pieces of glass were disposed in the cities where factories were located.

In this appendix, we will identify stretch glass pieces that have been presented in earlier works. We do this merely to assist in improving glass collectors' knowledge of this iridescent glass. We know fully well that many pieces in this book will likely be attributed to different manufacturers as more information comes to light. We welcome all new information as it becomes available.

IRIDESCENT STRETCH GLASS (1972, Kitty and Russell Umbraco)

This is the first book totally dedicated to stretch glass. Though out of print for many years, this book is occasionally available through book dealers. The Umbracos mention that Cambridge Glass Company made some stretch glass which we no longer believe to be true. They provide an extensive listing of colors that were known to them at the time. A 1974 – 75 price guide supplement was provided by the authors to people purchasing the book during that time period. They used a numbering system that included "KU" and a number. These numbers are used in the following listing:

KU1	Diamond tall trumpet candlesticks	KU28	Fenton #202 ash tray (w/o inserts)
KU2	Fenton #400 crimped vase	KU29	Northwood #647 bowl
KU3	Fenton #643 salver compote	KU30	Fenton #103 plate
KU4	Fenton flared vase	KU31	U.S. Glass #151 candlestick
KU5	Fenton #647 bowl with Decoration No. 2	KU32	U.S. Glass #310 candy jar base
KU6	Fenton #611 cupped vase	KU33	Northwood #301 plate
KU7	Fenton stippled rays comport	KU34	Northwood cheese dish
KU8	Northwood tree of life bowl	KU35	Fenton #643 covered bonbon
KU9	Fenton #847 melon rib bowl	KU36	Benzer (Diamond?) car vase
KU10	Fenton #249 candlesticks	KU37	Northwood cheese dish
KU11	Fenton #932 mayonnaise	KU38	Fenton #66 lemon tray
KU12	Fenton #312 footed bowl	KU39	Northwood? plate
KU13	Northwood tree of life tray	KU40	U.S. Glass #179 vase (foot ground off)
KU14	Fenton #570 fan vase	KU41	Fenton #66 lemon tray
KU15	Fenton #847 melon rib bowl	KU42	U.S. Glass cheese & cracker plate
KU16	Fenton #932 mayonnaise	KU43	Fenton #737 candy jar
KU17	Fenton nut cup	KU44	Fenton #735 candy jar base
KU18	U.S. Glass #15179 low foot comport	KU45	Fenton #316 candlestick
KU19	Diamond tumbler	KU46	Fenton #643 salver compote
KU20	Fenton #232 candlestick	KU47	Fenton #251 bud vase
KU21	Fenton laurel leaf plate	KU48	Fenton #636 candy jar base
KU22	U.S. Glass #310 high foot comport	KU49	Northwood #698 server
KU23	Fenton #638 plate	KU50	Fenton #106 bonbon
KU24	Northwood tree of life bowl	KU51	U.S. Glass #8076 open work bowl
KU25	Central rolled rim bowl	KU52	Imperial plate
KU26	Northwood #644 cupped comport	KU53	Northwood #682 footed bowl
KU27	Fenton #449 candlesticks	KU54	U.S. Glass bowl

KU55   Northwood #655 comport
KU56   Northwood or Fenton bowl
KU57   Northwood #642 bowl
         Fenton mayonnaise ladle
KU58   U.S. Glass vase
KU59   U.S. Glass plate
KU60   Fenton #640 bowl
KU61   Northwood #718 bowl
KU62   Fenton #318 candlestick
KU63   Northwood #649 bowl
KU64   Northwood tree of life comport
KU65   Fenton vase
KU66   Fenton #314 candlestick
KU67   Fenton #643 covered bonbon
KU68   Northwood #658 candlesticks
KU69   Fenton #647 bowl
KU70   Fenton #316 candlesticks
KU71   Fenton #647 bowl
KU72   Fenton bud vase
KU73   Benzer (Diamond?) car vase
KU71a Fenton? bowl
KU74   Fenton #640 bowl
KU75   Fenton #220 water set
KU76   Fenton #640 bowl
KU77   Fenton plate
KU78   Fenton #643 covered bonbon
KU79   Diamond candlestick/vase
KU80   Northwood bowl
KU81   Northwood bowl
KU82   Diamond cheese dish on Northwood plate
KU83   Northwood #669 bowl
KU84   Fenton #314 candlestick
KU85   Fenton #2006 bowl
KU86   Fenton? bowl
KU87   Fenton salt
KU88   Fenton salt
KU89   Fenton? or Diamond? bowl
KU90   Fenton #756 plate
KU91   Northwood #645 salver
KU92   ???
KU93   Diamond bowl
KU94   Fenton #655 cigarette box
KU95   Northwood #692 bowl
KU96   Fenton #318 candlesticks
KU97   Jeannette bowl
KU98   Fenton #556 cigarette holder
KU99   Fenton #1512 bowl
KU100 Jeannette plate
KU101 Fenton #848 bowl
KU102 Imperial plate
KU103 Jeannette bowl
KU104 Fenton #349 candlestick
KU105 Fenton #857 melon rib bowl
KU106 Imperial handled server
KU107 Lancaster handled server

KU108 Imperial plate
KU109 Imperial cheese dish on Lancaster plate
KU110 Imperial plate
KU111 Fenton?? bowl
KU112 Lancaster cheese dish
KU113 Lancaster candlesticks
KU114 Fenton bowl
KU115 Lancaster bowl
KU116 Lancaster bowl
KU117 Lancaster candlesticks
KU118 Lancaster bowl
KU119 Lancaster pea vase
KU120 Lancaster candlesticks
KU121 Lancaster comport
KU122 Lancaster plate
KU123 Fenton #401 night set base
KU124 Diamond stick/bowl
KU125 ???
KU126 Diamond candy jar
KU127 Fenton #8 candy jar base
KU128 Fenton #106 bonbon
KU129 Fenton #635 candy jar base
KU130 Fenton #8 candy jar
KU131 Fenton #743 puff jar
KU132 Fenton #550 footed bowl
KU133 Fenton #743 puff jar
KU134 Diamond candlesticks
KU135 Diamond? bowl
KU136 Northwood #659 candy jar
KU137 U.S. Glass #310 cheese & cracker set
KU138 Fenton puff jar
KU139 Fenton #260 high comport
KU140 Fenton #316 candlesticks
KU141 Fenton? bowl
KU142 Northwood #631 plate
KU143 Imperial double scroll candlestick
KU144 Northwood #649 bowl
KU145 Diamond candlestick
KU146 Northwood #654 comport
KU147 U.S. Glass plate
KU148 U.S. Glass hat vase
KU149 Diamond candlesticks
KU150 Diamond bowl
KU151 Fenton #1532A comport
KU152 Imperial plate
KU153 U.S. Glass #179 high foot comport
KU154 U.S. Glass plate
KU155 Fenton? bowl
KU156 Fenton #857 melon rib fan vase
KU157 Fenton #316 (early) candlestick
KU158 Fenton #857 melon rib bowl
KU159 Art glass vase
KU160 Imperial Art Glass bowl
KU162 Fenton bowl
KU163 Lancaster pea vase

KU164 Northwood tree of life tray
KU165 U.S. Glass bread plate
KU166 Fenton #847 melon rib fan vase
KU167 U.S. Glass candlestick
KU168 Imperial Art Glass bowl
KU168 Fenton #449 candlestick
KU169 Imperial Art Glass bowl
KU170 Imperial vase
KU171 U.S. Glass #314 comport
KU172 U.S. Glass #310 server
KU173 Imperial basket
KU174 Fenton #847 bowl
KU175 Imperial cheese dish
KU176 Fenton #1512 bowl
KU177 Diamond? or Fenton? bowl
KU178 Imperial vase
KU179 Imperial plate
KU180 Fenton #449 candlestick
KU181 Imperial heart handled server
KU182 Fenton #200 guest set
KU183 Fenton #318 candlestick
KU184 Fenton #314 candlestick
KU185 Fenton candlestick
KU186 Fenton #318 candlestick
KU187 U.S. Glass #310 plate
KU188 Fenton #1043 salver
KU189 U.S. Glass #310 plate

KU190 Fenton comport
KU191 Fenton #1502A handled server
KU192 Fenton #1561 handled server
KU193 Fenton #574 bonbon
KU194 Lancaster candy jar
KU195 Fenton #574 bonbon
KU196 Fenton #847 melon rib fan vase
KU197 Fenton #9 candy jar
KU198 U.S. Glass Pomona comport
KU199 Fenton #316 candlesticks
KU200 U.S. Glass #315 comport
KU201 Northwood tree of life comport
KU202 Imperial bowl
KU203 Fenton #2006 bowl
KU204 Fenton #640 bowl
KU205 Fenton #604 bowl

Supplement
KU75   Fenton #220 & 222 pitcher sets
KU40   U.S. Glass vase
KU123 Fenton #401 night set
KU205 Fenton #604 bowl, base and cup
KU19   Diamond pitcher & tumbler
KU206 Diamond Adam's rib pitcher & tumbler
KU207 Fenton pitcher & glass
KU168 Fenton cut ovals bowl
KU106 Imperial handled server

STRETCH IN COLOR (1972, Berry Wiggins)
    Berry Wiggins is a tireless researcher and educator. One of his first literary works was this book. Since its publishing, he has amassed one of the largest sets of research files on glass manufacturers in existence. In 1987, he produced a revised price guide and listed the correct manufacturer of the pieces which were illustrated in the book. Because this separate guide may be missing (if you are lucky enough to find this book), we list the correct identifications herein. (The pieces are listed per page, left to right, top to bottom.)

pg.13   Fenton #1663 console bowl
        Fenton #403 sherbet & plate
pg.15   Fenton #1532A comport
        Fenton #1561 handled oval tray
        Northwood cupped comport
        Northwood salver comport
        Northwood cupped bowl
        Northwood salver comport
pg.17   Central candlesticks
        U.S. Glass footed bowl
        U.S. Glass bell-twist candlesticks
        U.S. Glass #8076 open work bowl
pg.19   Fenton #847 melon rib bowl
        Fenton #847 melon rib fan vase
        U.S. Glass comport
        Fenton #1561 handled server
pg.21   Imperial comport
        Northwood #559 guest set
        Northwood #651 candlesticks

        U.S. Glass comport
pg.23   U.S. Glass #8076 open work bowl
        Fenton #640 bowl
        Fenton #550 footed bowl
pg.25   Imperial handled server
        Imperial cheese & cracker set
        U.S. Glass #8076 open work bowl
pg.27   Vineland #15 bowl
        Vineland #15 bowl
        Vineland #12 bowl
pg.29   Fenton #316 candlesticks
        Fenton #647 bowl
        Fenton #602 crimped vase
        Fenton #604 crimped bowl
        Fenton #602 vase
pg.31   Fenton #318 butter ball tray
        Lancaster comport
        Fenton #249 candlestick
        Fenton #349 cut oval candlesticks

IMPERIAL GLASS (1971, Richard and Wilma Ross)

This book emphasized the Imperial Free Hand line and Imperial Art Glass (Imperial Jewels). Though out of print, this book can be obtained from book dealers on a regular basis. The book has one of the best listing of Free Hand and many of the Art Glass pieces are illustrated. Plate X contains dark green (emerald green) pieces, Plates XI, XII, and XIII contain Pearl Amethyst and Pearl Silver pieces, Plates XIII, XIV, and XV contain Pearl Ruby (marigold), and Pearl White (crystal) pieces. Plate XV, middle row, contains two vases in marigold on milk (#1 & #3) and one vase in blue smoke on milk (#2). Plate XIX also has an excellent example of a vase with blue smoke on milk (bottom row, #3). Plate XXI illustrates an Imperial ruby plate (top row, #1).

DEPRESSION GLASS III (1976, Sandra McPhee Stout)

This book contains a variety of glasswares which are classed "Depression Era" though many pieces were made well before the Great Depression. Ms. Stout included numerous stretch glass pieces on Plates 15 and 16. Ms. Stout seems to have had access to U.S. Glass advertisements since her designations are generally correct.

Plate 15
1, 3 & 4.   Carnival glass
2.   Diamond footed comport
5.   Fenton #735 candy jar base
6.   Fenton? bowl
7.   Lancaster candy jar
8.   Fenton vase

9.   Lancaster candy jar base
10.   Fenton? bonbon
11.   Lancaster bowl
12.   Lancaster tall candy jar

Plate 16   All U.S. Glass
1.   Topaz #314 comport

2. Topaz #151 lily vase
3. Crystal #179 comport
4. Jade Green bowl
5. Topaz #314 bowl
6. Crystal #314 comport

7. Pink #310 console bowl
8. Crystal #8076 open work bowl
9. Blue #314 comport
10. Blue bowl

STANDARD ENCYCLOPEDIA OF CARNIVAL GLASS, 5TH EDITION (1996, Bill Edwards)

While this book is considered one of the "must haves" for carnival collectors, we find the lack of proper identification of stretch glass troublesome. While Mr. Edwards acknowledges pieces of stretch glass, he often mixes them in with true carnival glass which can be confusing to the novice collector. The following names used in the book are herein correctly attributed.

Adam's Rib – Diamond's #900 line was made in many colors and many pieces were decorated with enamel and some pieces were iridized with a stretch effect. Very few seem to have plain carnival iridescence.

Balloons – This is simply Imperial's decoration, Cut 12, which can be found on carnival iridized as well as stretch iridized pieces.

Barbella – This is a Northwood #700 tumbler. Northwood #688 tumblers are similar but with mold-formed handles. No pitchers are known by the authors though some were likely made. These are stretch lines.

Colonial – This appears to be Imperial's #600 line and Colonial was not used by Imperial for this line. Pitchers, tumblers, comports, and sherbets were made. Some have plain carnival iridescence but most have stretch iridescence.

Curtain Optic – Fenton's Curtain Optic and Rib Optic line pieces can be found with satiny iridescence. Both are claimed by stretch and carnival collectors.

Cut Ovals – Because most candlesticks do not change shape during their reheating, stretch marks are rarely well defined. However, Fenton placed these candlesticks in their Florentine Line (stretch glass), whether they had cut ovals or not.

Double Dolphin – Fenton originally placed these pieces in their Florentine Line and they are rightly considered stretch glass, even though they have the dolphins. This line also had triple dolphin pieces as well as diamond optic patterns.

Double Scroll – Imperial's #320 line consisted of a footed bowl and tall or short candlesticks. The bowl and tall sticks can be found with carnival or stretch iridescence. The candlesticks rarely display much stretch iridescence.

Floral and Optic – This Imperial pattern #5141 comes in numerous shapes (normal to cupped bowls to a flattened tray) and almost every color made by Imperial in the 1920s. Many pieces are obviously stretched while others have plain iridescence. This is a true crossover piece that has a floral pattern (typical of carnival) but was commonly given stretch iridescence.

Florentine – This name has been given to the common six-sided candlesticks made by Fenton, Northwood, and Vineland. In all cases, these appear to have been made during the period of stretch glass manufacture and these were placed in advertisements illustrating stretch glass. The term Florentine is a poor choice since this name can be confused with the Fenton Florentine Line (stretch glass).

Flower Pot – As far as we know, only Fenton made this pattern with concentric rings. Though some marigold pieces are known, iridized pieces with colored glass were generally given stretch iridescence.

Imperial Jewels Candle Holders – The illustrated candlesticks are Diamond's. Diamond made these in Ruby and Royal Lustre (ruby and cobalt blue) that have a shiny, mirror-like iridescence. Many others are found with excellent stretch iridescence. None have been seen with the Iron Cross mark of Imperial.

Jewels – We hope that this name will be forever stricken from the language of carnival and stretch glass collectors! However, being realists, we can only hope that Imperial Jewels will only be used to refer to the Imperial Art Glass Line, a line with heavy stretch effect applied to plain glass surfaces. The candlestick/bowl illustrated is from Diamond Glassware. Some are found with a plain marigold iridescence but most have excellent stretch iridescence.

Laurel Leaves – These octagonal plates, bowls, sherbets and mayonnaise pieces were made by Fenton. They were placed in the Fenton Florentine Line (stretch glass).

Smooth Panels – This simply refers to Imperial's considerably large line of vases with optic panels (numbers 6922, 6923, 6924, 6931,

6932, 6934, 6935, 6944, and 6945). These were often iridized and swung into various lengths. They can be found in every color that Imperial made and many received stretch iridescence.

Wide Panel (Imperial) – The illustrated candy jar base is a Diamond piece with stretch treatment. Most other authorities consider Imperial's Wide Panel to be an optic pattern (inside panels). This would include Imperial's #645, #647, #6569, and #6567 lines. These pieces are commonly found with stretch iridescence. Frankly, there seems to be little real difference between the optic patterns of these pieces and the Smooth Panels discussed above.

COLORED GLASSWARE OF THE DEPRESSION ERA 2 (1974, Hazel Marie Weatherman)

This monumental work contains hundreds of useful illustrations and copies of advertising pieces from numerous glass companies. We find the Imperial and Lancaster chapters especially useful for identification of items made by both companies. However, we caution readers of this book to disregard the names that have been superimposed (bold letters in quotes) over the various Imperial lines. These names were not used by the Imperial Company.

Useful References

Archer, Margaret and Douglas Archer. IMPERIAL GLASS. 1978. Collector Books, Paducah, KY. 226 pp.

Bickenheuser, Fred. TIFFIN GLASSMASTERS. 1979. Glassmasters Publications, Grove City, OH. 104 pp.

Bickenheuser, Fred. TIFFIN GLASSMASTERS, BOOK II. 1981. Glassmasters Publications, Grove City, OH. 160 pp.

Burns, Carl O. IMPERIAL CARNIVAL GLASS. 1996. Collector Books, Paducah, KY. 183 pp.

Heacock, William. FENTON GLASS, THE FIRST TWENTY-FIVE YEARS. 1978. O-Val Advertising Corp., Marietta, OH. 144 pp. (now: The Glass Press, Inc. dba Antique Publications, Marietta, OH.)

Heacock, William. Fenton Glass, THE SECOND TWENTY-FIVE YEARS. 1980. O-Val Advertising Corp., Marietta, OH. 156 pp. (now: The Glass Press, Inc. dba Antique Publications, Marietta, OH.)

Heacock, William, James Measell and Berry Wiggins. HARRY NORTHWOOD, THE WHEELING YEARS 1901 – 1925. 1991. Antique Publications, Marietta, OH.

Heacock, William, James Measell and Berry Wiggins. DUGAN/DIAMOND, THE STORY OF INDIANA, PENNSYLVANIA, GLASS. 1993. Antique Publications, Marietta, OH. 204 pp.

Measell, James (Ed.). FENTON GLASS, THE 1980S DECADE. 1996. The Glass Press, Inc., dba Antique Publications, Marietta, OH. 176 pp.

National Imperial Glass Collector's Society. IMPERIAL GLASS ENCYCLOPEDIA, VOLUME I, A- Cane. 1995. Ed.: James Measell, The Glass Press, Inc. dba Antique Publications, Marietta, OH. 226 pp.

National Imperial Glass Collector's Society. IMPERIAL GLASS ENCYCLOPEDIA, VOLUME II, Cape Cod – L. 1997. Ed.: James Measell, The Glass Press, Inc. dba Antique Publications, Marietta, OH. 494 pp.

Piña, Leslie and Jerry Gallagher. TIFFIN GLASS, 1914 – 1940. Schiffer Pub., Ltd., Atglen, PA. 191 pp.

Presznick, Rose. CARNIVAL AND IRIDESCENT GLASS, BOOK III. 1965. Banner Printing Co., Wadsworth, OH. 70 pp. + 87 pp. plts.

Ross, Richard and Wilma Ross. IMPERIAL GLASS, IMPERIAL JEWELS, FREE HAND, AND PRESSED GLASS. 1971. Wallace-Homestead Book Co., Des Moines, IA. 23 plates.

Stout, Sandra. DEPRESSION GLASS III. 1976. Wallace-Homestead Book Co., Des Moines, IA. 44 pp.

Umbraco, Kitty and Russell Umbraco. IRIDESCENT STRETCH GLASS. 1972. Cemba & Avery Publishers, Berkeley, CA. 62 pp. (with 1974 – 1975 supplement and price guide).

Weatherman, Hazel Marie. COLORED GLASSWARE OF THE DEPRESSION ERA 2. 1974. Weatherman Glassbooks, Ozark, MO. 401 pp.

Whitmyer, Margaret and Kenn Whitmyer. FENTON ART GLASS, 1907–1939. 1996. Collector Books, Paducah, KY. 320 pp.

Wiggins, Berry. STRETCH IN COLOR, BOOK 1. 1971. Berry Wiggins, Orange, VA. 48 pp.

Glossary

Blown-molded – glassware produced by placing a glob of molten glass onto the end of a blow tube. This "bubble" of glass is then placed into a mold and air is forced through the blow tube thereby forcing the glass into the shape of the mold.

Bonbon – a glass piece, often with a lid, used to serve sweets.

Card Tray – a flattened tray for taking calling cards. Most card trays from the stretch glass period have a flattened tray with no upturned rim and a stemmed foot.

Carnival Glass – a pressed or blown-molded glass that usually has patterns (geometric designs, plants or animals) and is shaped before being sprayed with a metallic salt mix to produce an iridescent finish.

Comport – another name for compote.

Compote – a bowl with a base and stem, sometimes with a cover, from which fruits, nuts or sweets are served.

Console Set – a set consisting of a bowl and two candlesticks that was intended to be used as a centerpiece on a table or buffet.

Cutoff Tail – linear mark left in surface of glass caused by cutting of molten glass gather that has been allowed to drop into a mold. Sometimes called a "straw mark" and often mistaken for a crack in the glass.

Dope – a metallic salt, usually of iron, aluminum or zinc, dissolved in a weak acid solution which is sprayed onto very hot glass which produces a shiny mirror-like or iridescent effect.

Doped Ware – glassware that has been sprayed with a metallic salt while still hot. This produces glassware that is now referred to as carnival, stretch or lustre glass.

Gather – the glob of molten glass rolled onto a metal rod, taken from the holding tank to the mold.

Glue Chip Decoration – a special glue is applied to cool glass which is then heated in an oven. The glue peels off irregular slivers of glass. The resulting glass surface looks like the pattern seen when frost forms on glass.

Ground Marie – usually a small holding marie that is ground off after the glass piece is finished. This mark looks like a pontil mark.

Iridescence – a surface that splits light into its component wave lengths and reflects a color or several colors.

Lehr – an annealing oven. A long oven containing a conveyer belt on which newly formed glass is allowed to cool very slowly to remove internal stresses.

Luster or Lustre – a metallic glaze or coating that produces a brilliant or iridescent surface.

Marie – the foot of a piece of glass, usually with a rim, that allows for a holder to grip the glass for handling and/or shaping.

Nappy – a shallow, open serving dish. Glass companies used the term rather loosely; some nappies have handles or crimped rims.

Optic Pattern – a term referring to a pattern made in the glass surface that is to be viewed through the other surface of the glass. Ring optic, diamond optic, and wide panels are common optic patterns seen in stretch glass.

Pontil Mark – the place on a handmade piece of glass where a metal rod is attached to the piece for ease of handling. When the rod is removed, an attachment scar remains. This scar may be left rough or ground down to a smooth circle.

Press-molded – glassware produced by placing molten glass into a mold and forcing the glass into the mold shape with a metal plunger.

Salver – a tray, often footed, for serving food. Most salvers from the stretch glass period have a flattened tray with an upturned rim and a stemmed foot.

Slag Glass – a non-uniform mixture of two or more colors of glass, usually opaque or translucent in effect.

Snap – a metal rod with clamps on one end that hold the marie of a piece of glass.

Stretch Glass – a pressed or blown-molded glass that has little or no pattern and is sprayed with a metallic salt mix while hot to produce an iridescent finish. This iridescent glass is reheated and usually reshaped which produces a cobweb iridescence (the stretch marks).

Stuck Up – a term used in glass making when the foot of a piece of glass is heat-attached to a metal plate that is attached to a metal rod. After handling and/or shaping, the glass is detached and the rough edge is ground smooth. Also called a ground foot.

Vaseline – a modern term commonly used by glass collectors to refer to yellow to yellow-green glass that receives its color from uranium-containing compounds. Fluorescent with a yellow glow under ultraviolet light (black light).

Index

COLLECTOR BOOKS

Informing Today's Collector

For over two decades we have been keeping collectors informed on trends and values in all fields of antiques and collectibles.

DOLLS, FIGURES & TEDDY BEARS

4707	A Decade of **Barbie** Dolls & Collectibles, 1981–1991, Summers	$19.95
4631	**Barbie** Doll Boom, 1986–1995, Augustyniak	$18.95
2079	**Barbie** Doll Fashion, Volume I, Eames	$24.95
4846	**Barbie** Doll Fashion, Volume II, Eames	$24.95
3957	**Barbie** Exclusives, Rana	$18.95
4632	**Barbie** Exclusives, Book II, Rana	$18.95
4557	**Barbie**, The First 30 Years, Deutsch	$24.95
4847	**Barbie** Years, 1959–1995, 2nd Ed., Olds	$17.95
3310	**Black Dolls**, 1820–1991, Perkins	$17.95
3873	**Black Dolls**, Book II, Perkins	$17.95
3810	**Chatty Cathy Dolls**, Lewis	$15.95
1529	Collector's Encyclopedia of **Barbie** Dolls, DeWein	$19.95
4882	Collector's Encyclopedia of **Barbie** Doll Exclusives and More, Augustyniak	$19.95
2211	Collector's Encyclopedia of **Madame Alexander Dolls**, Smith	$24.95
4863	Collector's Encyclopedia of **Vogue Dolls**, Izen/Stover	$29.95
3967	Collector's Guide to **Trolls**, Peterson	$19.95
4571	**Liddle Kiddles**, Identification & Value Guide, Langford	$18.95
3826	Story of **Barbie**, Westenhouser	$19.95
1513	**Teddy Bears & Steiff** Animals, Mandel	$9.95
1817	**Teddy Bears & Steiff** Animals, 2nd Series, Mandel	$19.95
2084	**Teddy Bears, Annalee's & Steiff** Animals, 3rd Series, Mandel	$19.95
1808	Wonder of **Barbie**, Manos	$9.95
1430	World of **Barbie** Dolls, Manos	$9.95
4880	World of **Raggedy Ann** Collectibles, Avery	$24.95

TOYS, MARBLES & CHRISTMAS COLLECTIBLES

3427	**Advertising Character** Collectibles, Dotz	$17.95
2333	Antique & Collector's **Marbles**, 3rd Ed., Grist	$9.95
3827	Antique & Collector's **Toys**, 1870–1950, Longest	$24.95
3956	Baby Boomer **Games**, Identification & Value Guide, Polizzi	$24.95
4934	**Breyer Animal** Collector's Guide, Identification and Values, Browell	$19.95
3717	**Christmas** Collectibles, 2nd Edition, Whitmyer	$24.95
4976	**Christmas** Ornaments, Lights & Decorations, Johnson	$24.95
4737	**Christmas** Ornaments, Lights & Decorations, Vol. II, Johnson	$24.95
4739	**Christmas** Ornaments, Lights & Decorations, Vol. III, Johnson	$24.95
4649	Classic Plastic **Model Kits**, Polizzi	$24.95
4559	Collectible **Action Figures**, 2nd Ed., Manos	$17.95
3874	Collectible Coca-Cola Toy **Trucks**, deCourtivron	$24.95
2338	Collector's Encyclopedia of **Disneyana**, Longest, Stern	$24.95
4958	Collector's Guide to **Battery Toys**, Hultzman	$19.95
4639	Collector's Guide to **Diecast Toys & Scale Models**, Johnson	$19.95
4651	Collector's Guide to **Tinker Toys**, Strange	$18.95
4566	Collector's Guide to **Tootsietoys**, 2nd Ed., Richter	$19.95
4720	The Golden Age of **Automotive Toys**, 1925–1941, Hutchison/Johnson	$24.95
3436	Grist's Big Book of **Marbles**	$19.95
3970	Grist's Machine-Made & Contemporary **Marbles**, 2nd Ed.	$9.95
4723	**Matchbox** Toys, 1947 to 1996, 2nd Ed., Johnson	$18.95
4871	**McDonald's Collectibles**, Henriques/DuVall	$19.95
1540	**Modern Toys** 1930–1980, Baker	$19.95
3888	**Motorcycle** Toys, Antique & Contemporary, Gentry/Downs	$18.95
4953	Schroeder's Collectible **Toys**, Antique to Modern Price Guide, 4th Ed.	$17.95
1886	Stern's Guide to **Disney** Collectibles	$14.95
2139	Stern's Guide to **Disney** Collectibles, 2nd Series	$14.95
3975	Stern's Guide to **Disney** Collectibles, 3rd Series	$18.95
2028	**Toys**, Antique & Collectible, Longest	$14.95
3979	**Zany Characters** of the Ad World, Lamphier	$16.95

FURNITURE

1457	American **Oak** Furniture, McNerney	$9.95
3716	American **Oak** Furniture, Book II, McNerney	$12.95
1118	Antique **Oak** Furniture, Hill	$7.95
2271	Collector's Encyclopedia of **American** Furniture, Vol. II, Swedberg	$24.95
3720	Collector's Encyclopedia of **American** Furniture, Vol. III, Swedberg	$24.95
3878	Collector's Guide to **Oak** Furniture, George	$12.95
1755	Furniture of the **Depression Era**, Swedberg	$19.95
3906	**Heywood-Wakefield** Modern Furniture, Rouland	$18.95

1885	**Victorian** Furniture, Our American Heritage, McNerney	$9.95
3829	**Victorian** Furniture, Our American Heritage, Book II, McNerney	$9.95

JEWELRY, HATPINS, WATCHES & PURSES

1712	Antique & Collector's **Thimbles** & Accessories, Mathis	$19.95
1748	Antique **Purses**, Revised Second Ed., Holiner	$19.95
1278	Art Nouveau & Art Deco **Jewelry**, Baker	$9.95
4850	Collectible **Costume Jewelry**, Simonds	$24.95
3875	Collecting Antique **Stickpins**, Kerins	$16.95
3722	Collector's Ency. of **Compacts, Carryalls & Face Powder Boxes**, Mueller	$24.95
4854	Collector's Ency. of **Compacts, Carryalls & Face Powder Boxes**, Vol. II	$24.95
4940	**Costume Jewelry**, A Practical Handbook & Value Guide, Rezazadeh	$24.95
1716	Fifty Years of Collectible **Fashion Jewelry**, 1925–1975, Baker	$19.95
1424	**Hatpins** & Hatpin Holders, Baker	$9.95
4570	Ladies' **Compacts**, Gerson	$24.95
1181	100 Years of Collectible **Jewelry**, 1850–1950, Baker	$9.95
4729	**Sewing Tools** & Trinkets, Thompson	$24.95
2348	20th Century Fashionable Plastic **Jewelry**, Baker	$19.95
4878	Vintage & Contemporary **Purse Accessories**, Gerson	$24.95
3830	Vintage **Vanity Bags & Purses**, Gerson	$24.95

INDIANS, GUNS, KNIVES, TOOLS, PRIMITIVES

1868	Antique **Tools**, Our American Heritage, McNerney	$9.95
1426	**Arrowheads** & Projectile Points, Hothem	$7.95
4943	Field Guide to **Flint Arrowheads & Knives** of the North American Indian	$9.95
2279	**Indian Artifacts** of the Midwest, Hothem	$14.95
3885	**Indian Artifacts** of the Midwest, Book II, Hothem	$16.95
4870	**Indian Artifacts** of the Midwest, Book III, Hothem	$18.95
1964	**Indian Axes** & Related Stone Artifacts, Hothem	$14.95
2023	**Keen Kutter** Collectibles, Heuring	$14.95
4724	Modern **Guns**, Identification & Values, 11th Ed., Quertermous	$12.95
2164	**Primitives**, Our American Heritage, McNerney	$9.95
1759	**Primitives**, Our American Heritage, 2nd Series, McNerney	$14.95
4730	Standard **Knife** Collector's Guide, 3rd Ed., Ritchie & Stewart	$12.95

PAPER COLLECTIBLES & BOOKS

4633	**Big Little Books**, Jacobs	$18.95
4710	Collector's Guide to **Children's Books**, Jones	$18.95
1441	Collector's Guide to **Post Cards**, Wood	$9.95
2081	Guide to Collecting **Cookbooks**, Allen	$14.95
2080	Price Guide to **Cookbooks & Recipe Leaflets**, Dickinson	$9.95
3973	**Sheet Music** Reference & Price Guide, 2nd Ed., Pafik & Guiheen	$19.95
4654	**Victorian Trade Cards**, Historical Reference & Value Guide, Cheadle	$19.95
4733	**Whitman Juvenile Books**, Brown	$17.95

GLASSWARE

4561	Collectible **Drinking Glasses**, Chase & Kelly	$17.95
4642	Collectible **Glass Shoes**, Wheatley	$19.95
4937	Coll. **Glassware** from the 40s, 50s & 60s, 4th Ed., Florence	$19.95
1810	Collector's Encyclopedia of **American Art Glass**, Shuman	$29.95
4938	Collector's Encyclopedia of **Depression Glass**, 13th Ed., Florence	$19.95
1961	Collector's Encyclopedia of **Fry Glassware**, Fry Glass Society	$24.95
1664	Collector's Encyclopedia of **Heisey Glass**, 1925–1938, Bredehoft	$24.95
3905	Collector's Encyclopedia of **Milk Glass**, Newbound	$24.95
4936	Collector's Guide to **Candy Containers**, Dezso/Poirier	$19.95
4564	**Crackle Glass**, Weitman	$19.95
4941	**Crackle Glass**, Book II, Weitman	$19.95
2275	**Czechoslovakian Glass** and Collectibles, Barta/Rose	$16.95
4714	**Czechoslovakian Glass** and Collectibles, Book II, Barta/Rose	$16.95
4716	**Elegant Glassware** of the Depression Era, 7th Ed., Florence	$19.95
1380	Encylopedia of **Pattern Glass**, McClain	$12.95
3981	Ever's Standard **Cut Glass** Value Guide	$12.95
4659	**Fenton** Art Glass, 1907–1939, Whitmyer	$24.95
3725	**Fostoria**, Pressed, Blown & Hand Molded Shapes, Kerr	$24.95
4719	**Fostoria**, Etched, Carved & Cut Designs, Vol. II, Kerr	$24.95
3883	**Fostoria Stemware**, The Crystal for America, Long & Seate	$24.95
4644	**Imperial Carnival Glass**, Burns	$18.95
3886	**Kitchen Glassware** of the Depression Years, 5th Ed., Florence	$19.95

COLLECTOR BOOKS
Informing Today's Collector

4725	Pocket Guide to **Depression Glass**, 10th Ed., Florence	$9.95
5035	Standard Encyclopedia of **Carnival Glass**, 6th Ed., Edwards/Carwile	$24.95
5036	Standard **Carnival Glass** Price Guide, 11th Ed., Edwards/Carwile	$9.95
4875	Standard Encyclopedia of **Opalescent Glass**, 2nd ed., Edwards	$19.95
4731	**Stemware Identification**, Featuring Cordials with Values, Florence	$24.95
3326	**Very Rare Glassware** of the Depression Years, 3rd Series, Florence	$24.95
4732	**Very Rare Glassware** of the Depression Years, 5th Series, Florence	$24.95
4656	**Westmoreland Glass**, Wilson	$24.95

POTTERY

4927	**ABC Plates & Mugs**, Lindsay	$24.95
4929	**American Art Pottery**, Sigafoose	$24.95
4630	**American Limoges**, Limoges	$24.95
1312	**Blue & White Stoneware**, McNerney	$9.95
1958	So. Potteries **Blue Ridge Dinnerware**, 3rd Ed., Newbound	$14.95
1959	**Blue Willow**, 2nd Ed., Gaston	$14.95
4848	Ceramic **Coin Banks**, Stoddard	$19.95
4851	Collectible **Cups & Saucers**, Harran	$18.95
4709	Collectible **Kay Finch**, Biography, Identification & Values, Martinez/Frick	$18.95
1373	Collector's Encyclopedia of **American Dinnerware**, Cunningham	$24.95
4931	Collector's Encyclopedia of **Bauer Pottery**, Chipman	$24.95
3815	Collector's Encyclopedia of **Blue Ridge Dinnerware**, Newbound	$19.95
4932	Collector's Encyclopedia of **Blue Ridge Dinnerware**, Vol. II, Newbound	$24.95
4658	Collector's Encyclopedia of **Brush-McCoy Pottery**, Huxford	$24.95
2272	Collector's Encyclopedia of **California Pottery**, Chipman	$24.95
3811	Collector's Encyclopedia of **Colorado Pottery**, Carlton	$24.95
2133	Collector's Encyclopedia of **Cookie Jars**, Roerig	$24.95
3723	Collector's Encyclopedia of **Cookie Jars**, Book II, Roerig	$24.95
4939	Collector's Encyclopedia of **Cookie Jars**, Book III, Roerig	$24.95
4638	Collector's Encyclopedia of **Dakota Potteries**, Dommel	$24.95
5040	Collector's Encyclopedia of **Fiesta**, 8th Ed., Huxford	$19.95
4718	Collector's Encyclopedia of **Figural Planters & Vases**, Newbound	$19.95
3961	Collector's Encyclopedia of **Early Noritake**, Alden	$24.95
1439	Collector's Encyclopedia of **Flow Blue China**, Gaston	$19.95
3812	Collector's Encyclopedia of **Flow Blue China**, 2nd Ed., Gaston	$24.95
3813	Collector's Encyclopedia of **Hall China**, 2nd Ed., Whitmyer	$24.95
3431	Collector's Encyclopedia of **Homer Laughlin China**, Jasper	$24.95
1276	Collector's Encyclopedia of **Hull Pottery**, Roberts	$19.95
3962	Collector's Encyclopedia of **Lefton China**, DeLozier	$19.95
4855	Collector's Encyclopedia of **Lefton China**, Book II, DeLozier	$19.95
2210	Collector's Encyclopedia of **Limoges Porcelain**, 2nd Ed., Gaston	$24.95
2334	Collector's Encyclopedia of **Majolica Pottery**, Katz-Marks	$19.95
1358	Collector's Encyclopedia of **McCoy Pottery**, Huxford	$19.95
3963	Collector's Encyclopedia of **Metlox Potteries**, Gibbs Jr.	$24.95
3837	Collector's Encyclopedia of **Nippon Porcelain**, Van Patten	$24.95
2089	Collector's Ency. of **Nippon Porcelain**, 2nd Series, Van Patten	$24.95
1665	Collector's Ency. of **Nippon Porcelain**, 3rd Series, Van Patten	$24.95
4712	Collector's Ency. of **Nippon Porcelain**, 4th Series, Van Patten	$24.95
1447	Collector's Encyclopedia of **Noritake**, Van Patten	$19.95
3432	Collector's Encyclopedia of **Noritake**, 2nd Series, Van Patten	$24.95
1037	Collector's Encyclopedia of **Occupied Japan**, 1st Series, Florence	$14.95
1038	Collector's Encyclopedia of **Occupied Japan**, 2nd Series, Florence	$14.95
2088	Collector's Encyclopedia of **Occupied Japan**, 3rd Series, Florence	$14.95
2019	Collector's Encyclopedia of **Occupied Japan**, 4th Series, Florence	$14.95
2335	Collector's Encyclopedia of **Occupied Japan**, 5th Series, Florence	$14.95
4951	Collector's Encyclopedia of **Old Ivory China**, Hillman	$24.95
3964	Collector's Encyclopedia of **Pickard China**, Reed	$24.95
3877	Collector's Encyclopedia of **R.S. Prussia**, 4th Series, Gaston	$24.95
1034	Collector's Encyclopedia of **Roseville Pottery**, Huxford	$19.95
1035	Collector's Encyclopedia of **Roseville Pottery**, 2nd Ed., Huxford	$19.95
4856	Collector's Encyclopedia of **Russel Wright**, 2nd Ed., Kerr	$24.95
4713	Collector's Encyclopedia of **Salt Glaze Stoneware**, Taylor/Lowrance	$24.95
3314	Collector's Encyclopedia of **Van Briggle** Art Pottery, Sasicki	$24.95
4563	Collector's Encyclopedia of **Wall Pockets**, Newbound	$19.95
2111	Collector's Encyclopedia of **Weller Pottery**, Huxford	$29.95
3876	Collector's Guide to **Lu-Ray Pastels**, Meehan	$18.95
3814	Collector's Guide to **Made in Japan** Ceramics, White	$18.95
4646	Collector's Guide to **Made in Japan** Ceramics, Book II, White	$18.95
4565	Collector's Guide to **Rockingham**, The Enduring Ware, Brewer	$14.95
2339	Collector's Guide to **Shawnee Pottery**, Vanderbilt	$19.95
1425	**Cookie Jars**, Westfall	$9.95

3440	**Cookie Jars**, Book II, Westfall	$19.95
4924	Figural & Novelty **Salt & Pepper Shakers**, 2nd Series, Davern	$24.95
2379	Lehner's Ency. of **U.S. Marks** on Pottery, Porcelain & China	$24.95
4722	**McCoy Pottery**, Collector's Reference & Value Guide, Hanson/Nissen	$19.95
3825	**Purinton Pottery**, Morris	$24.95
4726	**Red Wing Art Pottery**, 1920s–1960s, Dollen	$19.95
1670	**Red Wing Collectibles**, DePasquale	$9.95
1440	**Red Wing Stoneware**, DePasquale	$9.95
1632	**Salt & Pepper Shakers**, Guarnaccia	$9.95
5091	**Salt & Pepper Shakers** II, Guarnaccia	$18.95
2220	**Salt & Pepper Shakers** III, Guarnaccia	$14.95
3443	**Salt & Pepper Shakers** IV, Guarnaccia	$18.95
3738	**Shawnee Pottery**, Mangus	$24.95
4629	Turn of the Century **American Dinnerware**, 1880s–1920s, Jasper	$24.95
4572	**Wall Pockets** of the Past, Perkins	$17.95
3327	**Watt Pottery** – Identification & Value Guide, Morris	$19.95

OTHER COLLECTIBLES

4704	Antique & Collectible **Buttons**, Wisniewski	$19.95
2269	Antique **Brass & Copper** Collectibles, Gaston	$16.95
1880	Antique **Iron**, McNerney	$9.95
3872	Antique **Tins**, Dodge	$24.95
4845	Antique **Typewriters & Office Collectibles**, Rehr	$19.95
1714	**Black** Collectibles, Gibbs	$19.95
1128	**Bottle** Pricing Guide, 3rd Ed., Cleveland	$7.95
4636	**Celluloid Collectibles**, Dunn	$14.95
3718	Collectible **Aluminum**, Grist	$16.95
3445	Collectible **Cats**, An Identification & Value Guide, Fyke	$18.95
4560	Collectible **Cats**, An Identification & Value Guide, Book II, Fyke	$19.95
4852	Collectible **Compact Disc** Price Guide 2, Cooper	$17.95
2018	Collector's Encyclopedia of **Granite Ware**, Greguire	$24.95
3430	Collector's Encyclopedia of **Granite Ware**, Book 2, Greguire	$24.95
4705	Collector's Guide to **Antique Radios**, 4th Ed., Bunis	$18.95
3880	Collector's Guide to **Cigarette Lighters**, Flanagan	$17.95
4637	Collector's Guide to **Cigarette Lighers**, Book II, Flanagan	$17.95
4942	Collector's Guide to **Don Winton Designs**, Ellis	$19.95
3966	Collector's Guide to **Inkwells**, Identification & Values, Badders	$18.95
4947	Collector's Guide to **Inkwells**, Book II, Badders	$19.95
4948	Collector's Guide to **Letter Openers**, Grist	$19.95
4862	Collector's Guide to **Toasters** & Accessories, Greguire	$19.95
4652	Collector's Guide to **Transistor Radios**, 2nd Ed., Bunis	$16.95
4653	Collector's Guide to **TV Memorabilia**, 1960s–1970s, Davis/Morgan	$24.95
4864	Collector's Guide to **Wallace Nutting Pictures**, Ivankovich	$18.95
1629	**Doorstops**, Identification & Values, Bertoia	$9.95
4567	Figural **Napkin Rings**, Gottschalk & Whitson	$18.95
4717	Figural **Nodders**, Includes Bobbin' Heads and Swayers, Irtz	$19.95
3968	**Fishing Lure** Collectibles, Murphy/Edmisten	$24.95
4867	**Flea Market Trader**, 11th Ed., Huxford	$9.95
4944	**Flue Covers**, Collector's Value Guide, Meckley	$12.95
4945	**G-Men and FBI Toys** and Collectibles, Whitworth	$18.95
5043	**Garage Sale & Flea Market Annual**, 6th Ed.	$19.95
3819	**General Store Collectibles**, Wilson	$24.95
4643	**Great American West** Collectibles, Wilson	$24.95
2215	Goldstein's **Coca-Cola** Collectibles	$16.95
3884	Huxford's **Collectible Advertising**, 2nd Ed.	$24.95
2216	**Kitchen Antiques**, 1790–1940, McNerney	$14.95
4950	The **Lone Ranger**, Collector's Reference & Value Guide, Felbinger	$18.95
2026	**Railroad** Collectibles, 4th Ed., Baker	$14.95
4949	**Schroeder's Antiques Price Guide**, 16th Ed., Huxford	$12.95
5007	**Silverplated Flatware**, Revised 4th Edition, Hagan	$18.95
1922	Standard **Old Bottle** Price Guide, Sellari	$14.95
4708	**Summers' Guide to Coca-Cola**	$19.95
4952	Summers' Pocket Guide to **Coca-Cola** Identifications	$9.95
3892	**Toy & Miniature Sewing Machines**, Thomas	$18.95
4876	**Toy & Miniature Sewing Machines**, Book II, Thomas	$24.95
3828	Value Guide to **Advertising Memorabilia**, Summers	$18.95
3977	Value Guide to **Gas Station** Memorabilia, Summers & Priddy	$24.95
4877	Vintage **Bar Ware**, Visakay	$24.95
4935	The W.F. Cody **Buffalo Bill** Collector's Guide with Values	$24.95
4879	**Wanted to Buy**, 6th Edition	$9.95

This is only a partial listing of the books on antiques that are available from Collector Books. All books are well illustrated and contain current values. Most of these books are available from your local bookseller, antique dealer, or public library. If you are unable to locate certain titles in your area, you may order by mail from COLLECTOR BOOKS, P.O. Box 3009, Paducah, KY 42002-3009. Customers with Visa, Discover or MasterCard may phone in orders from 7:00–5:00 CST, Monday–Friday, Toll Free 1-800-626-5420. Add $2.00 for postage for the first book ordered and $0.30 for each additional book. Include item number, title, and price when ordering. Allow 14 to 21 days for delivery.

Schroeder's ANTIQUES Price Guide

. . . is the #1 best-selling antiques & collectibles value guide on the market today, and here's why . . .

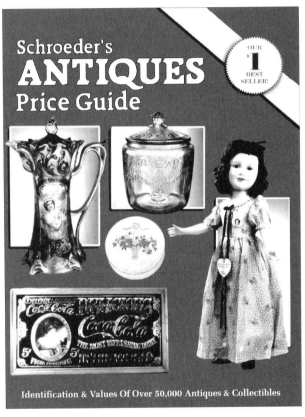

Schroeder's ANTIQUES Price Guide

OUR #1 BEST SELLER!

Identification & Values Of Over 50,000 Antiques & Collectibles

8½ x 11, 608 Pages, $12.95

• *More than 450 advisors, well-known dealers, and top-notch collectors work together with our editors to bring you accurate information regarding pricing and identification.*

• *More than 45,000 items in almost 550 categories are listed along with hundreds of sharp original photos that illustrate not only the rare and unusual, but the common, popular collectibles as well.*

• *Each large close-up shot shows important details clearly. Every subject is represented with histories and background information, a feature not found in any of our competitors' publications.*

• *Our editors keep abreast of newly developing trends, often adding several new categories a year as the need arises.*

If it merits the interest of today's collector, you'll find it in *Schroeder's*. And you can feel confident that the information we publish is up to date and accurate. Our advisors thoroughly check each category to spot inconsistencies, listings that may not be entirely reflective of market dealings, and lines too vague to be of merit. Only the best of the lot remains for publication.

Without doubt, you'll find
SCHROEDER'S ANTIQUES PRICE GUIDE
the only one to buy for
reliable information and values.

COLLECTOR BOOKS
A Division of Schroeder Publishing Co., Inc.